Letters From the Headwaters

Poetry

aaron a. abeyta

Letters From the Headwaters

Poetry

aaron a. abeyta

Western
Press Books

Edited by John Hausdoerffer
Western Press Books
Gunnison, Colorado

ISBN: 978-1-60732-362-4 (paperback)
ISBN: 978-1-60732-363-1 (ebook)

Library of Congress Control Number: 2014943473
Published in the United States of America

Western Press Books
Gunnison, Colorado

The following poems appeared in *Colcha*, University Press of Colorado, 2001:

A Letter to Guillermo Concerning Why i Must Write; a letter from my journal to juan; A Letter to an Adopted Son; An Open Letter on December 20th

The following poems appeared in *As Orion Falls*, Ghost Road Press, 2005:

A Letter to the Headwaters from This Place; A Letter About Memory on my Abuelito's 87th Birthday; A Letter to K. Translating Spanish; A Letter to K. About Rain and Hammers; An Open Letter Upon Seeing the Stars In A New Way; A Letter to the Headwaters from the Sovereign Banks of the Conejos; A Letter for the Unidentified Mexican National Who Died at 5:00 p.m. Somewhere Between San Luis and Manassa, His Van Rolling 3¼ Times; a letter to Pablo about hope; A Letter to Guillermo, Having Missed His Call.

For
Michele & Rut,
Always.

TABLE OF CONTENTS

Editor's Note   ix

Foreword   xi

The Sky Knows Itself—Place

A Letter to the Headwaters from This Place   3

A Letter to Guillermo Concerning Why i Must Write   6

A Letter About Memory on my Abuelito's 87th Birthday   8

A Letter to K. Translating Spanish   10

A Letter to K. About Rain and Hammers   12

a letter from my journal to juan   14

What Innate Star Guided Her—Hope

A Letter to the Headwaters About Blackbirds, Hollow Core Doors
and Other Gifts   19

An Open Letter Upon Seeing the Stars In A New Way   23

To Whom It May Concern (Cami I):   25

A Letter to the Graduating Class of 2008, Coronado High School,
Gallina, New Mexico   28

A Letter to an Adopted Son   31

Cover Letter   32

A Letter, Of Sorts, To My Agapetos Somatiko Eidei   36

Staying is Losing—Outsiders

A Letter to the Headwaters from the Sovereign Banks of the Conejos   45

A Letter from the Confluence of a Very Old River, Ghosts,
and a Few Brief Moments of Light   48

A Letter to the Headwaters About Remembering My Father
   in the Future,   54

A Letter for the Unidentified Mexican National Who
   Died at 5:00 p.m. Somewhere Between San Luis and Manassa,
   His Van Rolling 3¼ Times   58

Some Measure of Mercy—Justice

A Letter to the Headwaters Regarding a Boy's Memory   63

To Whom It May Concern (Cami II):   67

A letter to the parents of the San Luis Valley   71

A Letter to the Headwaters from the Radical Center   78

a letter to Pablo about hope   81

Ella—The Land

A Letter to the Headwaters Concerning What is Not There   87

A Letter to Leopold Upon Reading "The River of the Mother of God"   90

An Open Letter on December 20th   98

It Is Our Imperfections—Resilience

A Letter to the Headwaters from My River Dream,   106

A Letter to Mumper from a 4:00 a.m. Campus   112

A letter to the Men of Troy Concerning the Nature of Joy   117

A Letter to the Men of Troy   121

A Letter to Guillermo, Having Missed His Call   124

A Letter to the Antonito High School Graduating Class of 2013
   Regarding Their Book of Dreams, Happiness
   and Other Perpetual Things   126

A Letter to the Men of Troy, Where I Explain A Few Things   131

A Letter Regarding the Palace of Lost Fish   136

Editor's Note

"Quite often I am left at a loss when asked to write about various Headwaters topics, their subjects often feeling as foreign as a splinter under the flesh." These were the opening words of a public letter from Aaron Abeyta to me, read at the end of the first Headwaters Conference I directed. Each fall, for over a decade, Aaron has embarked from his "last and defensible homeland" of Antonito, Colorado, for our fall event in Gunnison. He crosses the gold and tan Cochetopa Hills dividing the Gunnison and San Luis Valleys to share a letter that unsettles the mostly transient, mostly Anglo, relatively privileged audience with a "fierce and clawed" hope for his "broken and tattered heart of a home." Being the recipient of an open letter from Aaron Abeyta is an exercise in humility, the kind of humility that walks the knife-edge between self-criticism and empathy. But I quickly realized that this was not a letter to me. This was not even a letter to a conference audience or to an entire region. This was a letter asking humanity to reawaken "the overlooked place of myth, the four chambered homeland that is our human heart."

Humility encapsulates Aaron's core offering, not just for the sake of individuals, or conference directors, or the people of a region, but humility for an entire practice of place. The title of Aaron's annual letter, though, "Letters to the Headwaters," is too humble. Truly, each year Aaron writes a formative letter from the Headwaters. Hence this book, Letters from the Headwaters, in which each chapter opens with a letter "to" the Headwaters Conference but blows beyond his feeling of being the outsider's voice to reclaim the "heart of a home" in this ever-diversifying Southwest. There is often an unjust burden of proof in the West: those who have been here the longest and deepest carry the burden of proving their legitimacy to the future of this place. Aaron's letters are truly letters from the Headwaters, because they reject that unjust equation.

Although this is a book organized around sequential chapters on Place, Hope, Outsiders, Justice, The Land, and Resilience, and although each section opens with a letter to the Headwaters Conference that is then expanded with letters that gradually return Aaron to the center of his Headwaters homeland, this book is not organized as a deliberate argument. The letters before you offer more of an epistolary chapbook than a linear manifesto. They challenge us all to see ourselves from the perspective of a place, to "think like a mountain" in seeing our whole region and ourselves from the top of the bare, broad shoulders of San Antonio Mountain rising above Aaron's home.

My only suggestion to you as reader is to co-create meaning with Aaron as author, rather than to seek some static, objective "meaning" in each poetic letter. As a reader, please join the dialogue, with and beyond the letters. Please join the dialogue that emerges when many peoples and species and geographies transform a region into a place. In turn, I suspect that to learn how to read these letters—patiently, cyclically—is to learn something vital about how to transform a place into a homeland.

John Hausdoerffer
Director, Headwaters Project
Western State Colorado University

Foreword

i am here
where the faces become a two lane road
one whispers east
to the testimonial light of new day
the other tugs me west
toward the dying red sun of our past
     —from "bones of my people"

Dear Aaron,

A foreword, a word before, is supposed to say something to prepare readers for what they are about to read, maybe add a little context to the text. But because this is a book of letters, it seems fitting to write this as a letter to you, to let you as well as your readers know why I presume to put a word before your work.

A little context for your unsuspecting readers is one reason. I met you at an early "Headwaters" gathering, at what was then Western State College, now Western State Colorado University. The Headwaters gatherings were, and are, intended to be annual cross-disciplinary and cross-cultural conferences bringing students and faculty together with people from the region surrounding the university—a diverse, rugged, mostly spectacular and occasionally difficult, even indifferently cruel, region of mountains and valleys, mesas and canyons, high wet snow-catching peaks and high dry deserts. These mountains are the source of all the major rivers of the mostly-arid southwestern and lower midwestern United States, as well as northern Mexico—hence, a headwaters region.

In addition to its importance to the driest quadrant of the United States, this headwaters region is culturally unique in its own right: a cultural crossroads where Archaic Indians resided for at least 10,000 years, culminating in the extensive but mysteriously failed "Anasazi" civilization. Around the time of that collapse, other "first nations" moved into the region, some from far to the north, some probably Anasazi refugees. Then 400 years ago the headwaters of the Rio Grande and San Juan River became *El Norte* for Spanish-Americans expanding into the region from Mexico, first pushing against but eventually merging with the peoples already there —the merging that gave us you today. And finally, only 160-some years ago, Anglo-American "unsettlers," came into The West and eventually the headwaters and pushed everyone already there around in the innocent and arrogant way of those who believe they are fulfilling a destiny. Cultural tensions continue to simmer—sometimes ugly, but occasionally burbling up in the sublime irony of something like an "English Only" campaign in a region whose major features mostly bear Spanish and Indian names.

Many of those cultural roots remain in the region to some extent, and in-migrations keep happening: new waves of workers from Mexico, retirees and other refugees from the increasingly intemperate zones to the north and east, and new iterations of the adventurers, raconteurs, peddlers and other odd lots who keep the West and *El Norte* interesting.

How and why Western State Colorado University began to base some of its programs around the articulation, disciplined exploration and "voicing" of this headwaters region is an interesting story, but not for here. Suffice it to say that we first met you through an annual multi-disciplinary and cross-cultural gathering on "the headwaters campus of the Southwest/El Norte." These "headwaters conferences" over the past quarter-century have brought honored presenters to the headwaters, and many who deserve more honor than they have gotten for lives lived well in headwaters places. But none of them has more perfectly realized the vague ideas and, yes, somewhat romantic vision, at the heart of Western's "headwaters idea" than you, Aaron.

When we first heard you and your poetry, you were finishing up your Master of Fine Arts degree at Colorado State University. We learned that you were a native of a village that no longer exists, near Antonito in Colorado's San Luis Valley, and of a culture that is struggling to continue existing on some of its own terms, out of its own heritage, in the face of a powerful and indifferent dominant culture. Yours is a culture grounded in land and the water that gives life to the land, but in the international shenanigans after the Mexican War the cultural compass of the San Luis Valley was turned violently 90 degrees from south toward Mexico to east toward the United States. Your people lost much of their land (especially the valuable *ejido*, the commons), and much of the water that was needed to make the high dry valley productive, in a badly managed and sadly exploited transition from Hispano-American law and mores to Anglo-American.

None of this has been forgotten by the people of Antonito, nor by you. You graduated from Antonito High School and went on to college in the Northwest with a football scholarship, intending to forever shake the dust of the high dry *llanos* from your shoes. Exactly when and where you discovered you really had a serious poet's voice, I don't know, but I like to think it was about the same time that the high dry *llanos* and "the mountains named after blood" began to tug you back, and returning to the San Luis Valley became an important goal for you and your longtime partner Michele, also an Antonito native. After finishing at CSU, you began adjuncting at Adams State College in the San Luis Valley (now also a university), commuting the 30 miles from your old home town. Eventually Adams State recognized the gift and you became part of the full-time faculty; you and Michele are probably "home for good."

The idea of "letters from or to the Headwaters" grew out of your first or second appearance at a Headwaters gathering sometime in the 1990s; you read a prose-poem from your first book, *Colcha*: "Tierra," about gathering hay with your brother and *abuelito*, grandfather. It spoke of a place, not just as property or a piece of geography but as land that had been hallowed by the investment of generations past, keeping it as alive as possible for generations to come.

We asked: Could you maybe bring something like that to the Headwaters gatherings—well, forever? You said you would try. That was probably the early origin of this volume. Where it began, but not where you have taken it.

Wallace Stegner said that "no place is a place until things that have happened in it are remembered in history, ballads, yarns, legends, or monuments." He went on to conclude that "no place is a place until it has had a poet"—a poet who brings to the place "the kind of knowing that involves the senses, the memory, the history of a family or a tribe ... the knowledge of place that comes from working in it in all weathers, making a living from it, suffering from its catastrophes, loving its mornings or evenings and hot noons, valuing it for the profound investment of labor and feeling that you, your parents and grandparents, your all-but-unknown ancestors have put into it ... the knowing that poets specialize in."

We got that from you—bountifully and often unexpectedly. Most of us would have been happy enough with poetic renderings of loving *abuelitos* and *abuelitas*, heartwarming stories of multi-cultural melding. But what we got was frequently preceded by a statement like, "This year's theme is like a splinter under my skin"—followed by what sometimes seemed at first to be a complete diversion or perversion of our theme. But it always became your transformative challenge to think our theme through on other levels, beyond our own semi-conscious cultural box. "Sovereignty" was the theme? You brought us the story of a ne'er-do-well druggy who died in his forties, and made it the story of a person totally marginalized by the dominant/domineering culture but who carried forward—and passed on to you—his "sovereign excellence" as a fisherman. You bring to the headwaters gathering the voice of a people beaten down, but you assert their right, your right, to be not defeated. The true poet is not a historian, a recorder, but (as John Gardner said first and best) a shaper—one who "looks strange-eyed at the mindless world and turns dry sticks to gold."

I've thought a lot over the years about the idea of "headwaters"—the place where the water starts, and by extension, where life starts (we being just water that has figured out how to stand up, look around and think). It's a paraphrase of Stegner to say that we may not truly know who we are till we find the headwaters of our own lives, our people, our cumulative souls. But the headwaters is also always a hard place; the cultural people that come there eventually have to either grow a little humble and adapt their cultures to the place, or the rigors of the place eventually drive out the culture. The current dominant culture, totally dependent on the cities of the plain to survive in the headwaters, tries to ignore this reality— ignoring what you say in one of your letters: "Prosperity is just another way of saying temporary."

So some of your value to all of us, I think, is the way you are chronicling your own culture facing up to headwaters realities, tallying the beatings on the one hand, and on the other exhorting your young Trojans to keep alive what works in the place and to never be defeated, however often beaten. You are a man now at your own headwaters, and the San Luis Valley has become a place for many of us because it has its poet: a heart and mind mercilessly honest but always forgiving in seeing your place as it is, and its place in the world as it is today.

We need the poets that could tell with the same forgiving honesty the other sides of stories you tell, and we can hope that, following your example, they will emerge in our shared headwaters: showing that the future is best that carries forward the best of the past, with the often strange, mutated and wonderful sovereign excellence you shape and exemplify as our poet.

Tu amigo,
George Sibley

It is the work of writers to save, with our dreams and imagination,
what others relegate to the forgotten.
It is a writer's job, to connect what the heart knows to what the eyes see.
—From Aaron's letters

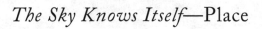

The Sky Knows Itself—Place

A Letter to the Headwaters from This Place

Dear George,

Here is this struggle, my struggle to write about a place when all i do is write about this place. Some part of me feels like all you have to do is press play and i will begin again in some innate migration to the llanos, mountains, churches and rivers that form my home. i suppose it is no accident that i chose the word migration. my people came to my valley home and lands of New Mexico over 400 years ago and have been stealing or stolen from ever since.

i tell my students that we are by nature a migratory people. our own migration is like Orion's, the constellation just now back in our night, and his winter journey through the sky. He begins himself, tilted in the east, lying on his side and moves slowly upright in the southern sky before falling again on his side in the west. And then there is my own abuelito who personified this for me, who fell into his western sky on February 15th at 1:35 p.m. By now you must be wondering what my many loose connections, stars, migration, religion, family are trying to do here. Ultimately, they must be together and will be my place.

George, here is how the connections come to me. i am six years old and my parents have moved us to Pueblo, where my dad has found work. Every weekend, and i mean every weekend, we load our Caprice Classic and we drive south to this place that is ours. Sometimes my older brothers have football games and we leave after, our headlights cutting through the early morning of a road filled with pot-holes, so that we can pull into the driveway of my boyhood home at three in the morning. Later, at six a.m., my father wakes us so that we can begin the ranch work which has been neglected during the week. The story unfolds from there, packing up Sunday evening and returning to Pueblo and a house where we all do not fit, my brothers sleeping in the family room.

To me the idea of a place, a sense of place is somewhere we come back to at all costs and at all hours of the day or night. i think often of the

Monarch butterflies and their yearly migration to the south where they will finally rest in the Mexican pines. i have heard that there are so many of them that the trees groan from the weight of so many butterflies, the thick branches bent toward the earth in supplication. Here is the tragic part. Every year fewer and fewer butterflies return to Mexico. They are victims of pesticides, growth and too many cars, much like us.

i mention the butterflies because they remind me of my town and how many of us return despite the poverty, and like the Monarchs fewer and fewer make the journey with each passing generation. My town is still poor, though every year the river canyon west of my home is gobbled up by homes made of beautiful scraps. The lumber which goes into the homes is standard grade, the same stuff that clogs canyons and shorelines everywhere so that someone can have a view. The scraps, those are measured in human terms. For the most part these transplants buy only the necessities from my town, gas and fishing licenses. We see very little of the wealth that grows three stories high on a ridge where pine and aspen used to mingle. We are a beautiful people that too many think of as scrap.

So back to the butterflies, may my God bless them and their journey. May this same God bless Orion and all the rest of us who travel so that we may return and rest in the warm trees that are innately part of us. All this rambling George, and essentially what i'm saying is that a place defines us because the soul and the home are synonymous.

One last thing amigo, earlier i mentioned my abuelito and his passing. His star is somewhere beyond the San Juans' grasp, fading slowly from this hemisphere and brilliantly into another. i mention him because i miss him and because i believed, and to a certain extent still do, that he is permanently a part of this place, my home, a mountain range away from yours. i never got to say goodbye to him, though i was at his bedside on that February afternoon when it seemed even the sheep in the field below his home stopped moving. The only thing in the air was his last breath and the mumbled prayers of someone speaking too fast in Spanish.

So you see George, there is no sense to goodbyes because our human mind will not let go what it knows will return. i see my abuelito at the table playing solitaire, chopping wood, driving off to the sheep camp or simply standing there broad shouldered. This too, memory, is our place, and this round home we call earth, she disappears from herself and from us at times but returns in whatever positions are native to her and our memory. These canyons that wrinkle her and the butterflies that fan her and rest in her hair keep coming, migrating toward us and through us or perhaps it is the other way around. We cannot say goodbye to our places, no matter how they change, we must always return to them. George we make each place our own by the things we return to it, living or remembered.

Much peace to you and your own place with its migrations uniquely yours. Please do share.

Be well.

your friend,
a.

A Letter to Guillermo Concerning Why i Must Write

Dear Guillermo,

i feel that i must write. That there is something inside me which, like always, needs to be said, needs to be told. i look back now on the stories of my little town. The town which i cannot leave, my heart somehow held within its adobe walls. i think of the time i tripped running across the street and saw deep grooves cut into the asphalt from all those years of cruising back and forth, by all those people young and old, all of whom i know by name. It is muscles flexed for full effect, smooth necks, long hair, well sprayed being tossed like bait. These are the arms which bring me back, the beauty which keeps me.

Guillermo, it is not about the grooves in the street. It is about how they got there. They were formed by age, sun, wind and all those forces of nature we writers substitute for love and metaphor.

i think about that town, old and brown like Lara's house, which a long time ago my brothers and i tore down, how that was our last attempt at leaving, how we didn't know then what the house stood for, what the town stood for. We did not realize that when we took our hammers and shovels to it we were trying to destroy a part of our past. i believed that because we were going to plant alfalfa where it stood this somehow made it all right to bring the house back to its roots of dust and memory.

i remember how we tore into that house and turned the adobe to a fine dust that clung to our skin like an old shirt. i remember that we listened to my abuelo as he told us that the field used to be more than just chamizo, how despite the rocks Lara had managed to plant grain. How now, despite the rocks, we must re-plant ourselves there.

Towards the end of the day we were tired. We had taken in all the stories my abuelito offered, and with each piece of the wall crumbling the names would disappear like willow flesh from our memories. Knowing that our own names would somehow be forgotten beneath the din of magpies that flew down from the cliffs to watch, to wait at the base of the mountain

6

where long ago some lover had painted two blue hearts, now fading. As we finished, our bodies tired, we were able to walk away. i was the last to leave, a soft stepper walking on the brown skeleton of Lara's house, leaving my own name with the crumbled walls so the magpies could finally eat.

A Letter About Memory on my Abuelito's 87th Birthday

So here is how i will remember this place, my father arm wrestling with his 87-year-old father.

"Let him win" someone says quietly, so that my abuelito will not hear.

"Viejo pero no espuelaio" he declares when he beats my father.

My abuelito defines this place, small house with thick adobe walls where my grandmother kept wild cats fed, almost loved.

From the kitchen window you can see the Mogotes, blue at dusk, just before dark. At this window my abuelo would shave in the early mornings, in almost this same light, slightly more orange and much quieter as he had the kitchen to himself. He is 87 now, and in his memory he claims to have seen the Conejos River from that window. Now there are trees, green now in summer, which twist along the vega marking the river's path. From this window you can see the broken down wagon which long ago he used to haul ice from the river. He tells Michele and i that sometimes he feels like his old wagon, missing wheels, boards missing, broken, or bowed with time.

It is approaching 9 p.m., almost time to put my grandfather to bed. He does not walk anymore. He has to be lifted from his wheelchair onto a small hospital bed which barely seems present in a room that used to be full of my abuelo and his history. When i was young he had a cabinet full of rifles, pistols, and a sword from the Spanish-American war. i admired the 30.30., the magnums, the .32 Beretta pistol, the massive sword which seemed to weigh more than the entire room. His room seems smaller now. The bed barely taking up space next to the north wall, the gun cabinet, unlocked, empty except for the dust and various canes. It was not always this way.

When i was young i would ride my bike, the ¼ mile west, to my grandparent's to chop wood for their wood stove. It was one of those chores a kid does because he is a kid, not because he can chop wood. My abuelito could chop wood better than any man i have ever seen. Holding the wood block with his left hand, his right arm ascending with a double adze blade, seven pounds, just above his head and then dropping quickly, like a blinking eye, inches away from the fingers of his left hand, the log splitting perfectly, one blow. Chopping wood is one of those talents which is almost lost to the world. Save for memory.

He was rarely home, always driving his Ford truck to some camp, some mountain. It is difficult to see him without motion. He is a nicer man now, but something in me longs for the meaner abuelito who struck fear in me as i admired him. i don't know, really, how to remember him, or if i should just know him as he is now. To remember or to know. Perhaps both.

So here is how i will remember this place. Just before dark with the sky blueing to black, my abuelito in a wheelchair, strong except for his legs. This kitchen with scuffed linoleum, my abuelito at his same spot, the head of the table, the empty chair to his left, my grandmother's place, empty for seven years now. The water from the well has always been cold and sweet. The window has always had a view of the vega, corral, the broken wagon at the bottom of the hill. There are only juice glasses in the cabinet; i leave the water running as i drink four glasses. My abuelito is behind me and to my left. He asks me if i remember this place, living here, my abuelita who always baked bread on Friday. i finish my last glass of water, turn the faucet shut. i turn to my grandpa, knowing that i will always remember this place.

"Yes." i say, and for a while this is when the room becomes silent, the night finally wins, and it is time for bed.

A Letter to K. Translating Spanish

i think it is interesting that you would mention such things as the valley sky, breath and cold now that Orion is wildly tilted in our eastern winter sky. He is my favorite constellation, though i do not know what he could be hunting in a sky so welcoming.

Recently i looked over some of my very old and not so good poems and noticed that i mentioned sky almost instinctively. i was fascinated with clouds, rain, snow and other things aviary like our owl. Later, i looked at the new stuff and noticed that the sky had left the poems. There was no mention of the fingernail moon, the clouds that arrive already bruised in late summer. Orion, every night, reminds me that the sky is what makes the valley. At first, i thought it was the mountains, the winter Blanca, Crestone and the San Juans. At one point i thought it was religion that defined the valley.

These things are still very much a part of me and this place Michele and i, again, call home.

The sky though. The mornings are my favorite, sunrise and all its shades of blues, blacks and reds. i said once that the sky in the mornings is a malignant blue. i don't think people understood what i meant by that; malignant is such a negative word, even for a sky that is immune to negativity. i did not mean that the sky would die of some disease, though some think it might, but rather that it grows from itself, multiplies in ways a pen, brush or imagination cannot fathom. Often, we do not know why things grow inside us. The sky knows itself very well i think. It grows with purpose.

So every night as Orion lies there in the winter east. i breathe a few visible breaths in his direction. i watch as the vapor ascends without the reservations of gravity. i can see the silhouetted hills and mountains against the light of the stars, millions of them.

Without the sky they would not be no mountains. i think maybe your student might have meant poner, as in to put light into a person's shoes.

Perhaps he meant for someone to walk like the stars, across the dark sky with all their lit shoes and bright eyes.

Para poner la luz en tu zapatos. That is quite nice.

i will tell our owl, Michele's good friend with the very white wings that stretch into the above mentioned sky, to look out for you and your good husband. So that you will know, she flies over an earth which is mostly brown, though it looks gold when the light is right. Just the other day the owl flew over a white earth, and that night as the frost formed on the wire fences around our home, in the headlights of our vehicle, the crystals of ice looked like stars, touchable and cold. The sky caught my breath that night, and Orion did not hunt.

Adios.

Your friend,

a.

A Letter to K. About Rain and Hammers

It sounds to me that you have found peace amidst the banging of a hammer and the dust of creating new things. There is much creation in you. Your house, garden, and friends do better with your attention. The roof will be a good thing for you to undertake. Perhaps there will be leak after a hard rain. Something tells me that if there is it will be a nice reminder of the hard work you put in.

i guess i think of leaks in a roof as a single flaw, necessary and mysterious. Origins with such things are not so easy to trace but worth looking into.

This last September i began to appreciate such things as leaks. Here is that story.

We were back in the valley after a long time away. This part you know, but we returned to daily rains and much green. This we were not used to, so much of two things in a place where we become used to brown. There were daily rains and we, one evening when the sky was especially full, decided to go to church.

i've told you about the priest who preaches nothing but Devil and damnation. This is a God story. The priest had begun. Again, he was talking about the fiery furnaces of hell, and then it began to rain.

The church, with its tin roof, sits in a meadow, very green and full this year. Beneath this tin roof there is a single, very small, room with a few wooden pews, an altar, some saints and Jesus on the wall, and at the front a priest.

It began to rain very hard. i smiled thinking it was angels, thousands of them, running across the tin roof. The drops of rain on the few windows liked the last of the autumn light and the church was filled with sound and that very same light. The priest worked hard to speak above the rain. Today the devil or whatever evil we were supposed to fear in this sermon succumbed to the rain.

i was happy.

Then, Karen, it was silent for a few seconds, the sermon and rain ending almost on cue. It is then that the roof betrayed its flaw, very fast dripping at the rear of the church. Here is where man shows his own flaws. From the old wooden rafters at the rear of the church, someone had tied an old coffee can with baling wire. This person had not sought out the source of the leak, a narrow slit, a small lightless hole where a nail had failed to do its job. Rather, this person had instead placed a coffee can, a tinny metronome to count the cadence of our meditation.

There is much sound in hammers, roofs, rain, and peoples' thoughts. The flaw is not always necessary, but it is a way to remember sound after the initial work has rested. You mentioned Lent. i think you said something of introspection. That is a carpenter's work and a writer's too. It is a good thing that you are both. A sound maker.

Sometimes it will take a dripping roof to make a person write. Other times it will be a well hammered note from a friend that you haven't heard from in a long time. Both are like the rain, proof of things beyond our own tracing, without origins, but in us like a tinny metronomic heartbeat.

peace, be well.

Your amigo,
a.

a letter from my journal to juan

writing from canada de los tankes
sheep have stopped here again
seems mythical how they know where to stop
do not miss city think of friends
but enjoy being alone

my abuelito used to measure everything in summers
this annual trip to sierra marked his existence
he was first to point out how sheep stop here on their own
have always loved that about this place good spirits
abuelito does not make trip anymore too old
wonder if he now learns seasons in reverse
marks his years with return of herd to rancho
assume this is the case
he would not know any other way

made a good pot of beans
had to add water six times
took eight hours to make them on the estufita
will savor them

rained the night before herd got here
had hard time making fire
thought of Pound real education must ultimately be limited to men
who insist on knowing. the rest is mere sheep-herding
never liked that guy
wonder if he knows what got into Ubaldo in 1957
wonder what made him leave his herd in the middle of the night
and run for six miles
before falling off the cliffs of toltec gorge
brujas

ezra might know
do not think he knows what it was like for sheep
lost 86 head
coyotes had a good winter
truly doubt if he knew the smell of Ubaldo's body
when my abuelito found him in river at bottom of gorge
he was only one able to carry him out
do not envy him
cannot imagine feel of skin falling off body
anyway back to pot of beans
had trouble with fire
wished Pound book had been in my possession

lost a borregito somewhere in brazos
must have tired
sheep did not seem to care
but noticed that her ubre was swelling
will begin summer in rincon bonito
where Gabriel killed six deer with six shots
amazing shots
beginning to understand why
if you ask a herder what he is doing
he usually replies making a pot of beans
live from meal to meal
can see that is how it works out here

mosquitoes are like bad dream which am unable to wake from
they tend to stick to the cool wet around the river
makes fishing difficult
but still enjoy the odd angles of my shadow on water
think of grandpa Joe
my last image of him

peaceful and somehow baggy as he stood beneath crab apple tree
odd memory
the baggy part
but knew he had died because of that image
remember him as good fisherman
beautiful unfurling of his line
bamboo rods lonely in garage after his death
think of him often on river
his spirit must be around here somewhere
always walking upstream
because that was the way he did it
can see him sometimes
good fisherman

must sign off for now
please wish everyone my love
take care
adios

What Innate Star Guided Her—Hope

A Letter to the Headwaters About Blackbirds, Hollow Core Doors and Other Gifts

Dear George,

Outside my window there are a few blackbirds perched in the dead branches of a Russian Olive. Presumably these birds, the approximate size of a human heart, are willing to tough out the Antonito winter. Later, when the snow falls, they will line the icy edge of the river, their black bodies set against the white. I've always been intrigued by these birds, wondering why they don't fly south like every other sane creature capable of migrating.

For now, everything here is brown. The grass died long ago, the leaves prior to that. My neighbor's roof is literally swaying in the wind, the loose tin flapping like the broken wing of a rusted bird. East of here, behind Sargents, an old and abandoned grocery store, there are millions of pieces of glass catching the November sun. Later, when it warms up a bit, the winos will venture onto the street and make their way to one of the liquor stores. Purchase in hand, they will sit street side, to the south of the old grocery store and they will drink their fortified liquor and when the last drop has left this world and entered their body, a world onto itself, they will take that bottle and leave it among its broken predecessors. Later, a car, a kid, or someone who is bored in a way that can only be brought on by poverty will break that bottle and the pieces of it will find their way into the kaleidoscope of broken glass.

Main street. Abandoned buildings. Roadside planters where no flower has grown in recent memory. Eight hundred people, give or take. Two liquor stores. Two full time bars and two others that will serve alcohol on special occasions. This is where I live. Perhaps it goes without saying, it is beautiful here.

Social capital. Honestly, I almost laughed when I heard that was the topic for this year's Headwaters. You'd think in a place as poor as Antonito that all we'd have left us is social capital. I'm not sure.

Here is how you can know a house. A hollow core door splintering and without paint, a yard filled with appliances, a car up on blocks, a woodpile of scrap lumber, front steps made of that very same lumber, windows with missing screens or screens ratted with holes and repaired with clear tape, a construction project left unfinished, the particle board curling up like paper put to flame, a fence made of wooden pallets, a sprinkler attempting the impossible, to keep alive a patch of grass. That grass, that hollow door, may all of it stand for hope.

At first I thought I'd begin a discussion on social capital by writing about a culture and language that are centuries old, or by revisiting the stories of elders whose lives are woven with myth and history, or perhaps I could write about the murals that bloom color onto walls and into our streets. Like I said, it's beautiful here. All of these would be social capital, I suppose.

Inside the high school there is a mural. We are the Antonito Trojans. The muralist painted the battle between Hector and Achilles. I believe in symbolism. Perhaps the body of my town was long ago tied to the back of a chariot and dragged away. Did the muralist know that over 100 kids would leave this school and go up the road to a "*better*" school where they will, for the most part, be rendered invisible? Every morning I pass the long line of cars at the district line as they wait for the bus. I want to stop and ask them which of the children that have left Antonito schools, which of the kids that have gone to this "*better*" school have made a beautiful and lasting mark in the world? Perhaps there are one or two. I cannot think of any. Can you leave the community where your ancestors dreamt you into existence and go 14 miles up the road where you've never lived and come away with anything that even remotely resembles social capital? Dear and beaten Hector tied to the back of every car that waits for that traitor of a yellow bus.

I am not a negative person. I love the world. Like Whitman, I believe that the human soul is always beautiful and that every soul is beautiful. Social capital. The optimistic soul as social capital. Perhaps. No. Today this cannot be.

Here I am, nearly halfway into this letter, and all I can come up with is this. Sometimes there is something greater than love, some wispy thing like pollen on a breeze that outweighs even the privilege of money. That thing? What heavy wood, full of pitch, stokes the burning within us and keeps us, even through our long winters, warm and in life? Resentment. Such a negative word you might say. Here, today, as I paint my own mural of sorts, I argue that sometimes you must find beauty where no one has sought to look.

I live in a beautiful place surrounded by three rivers, all of which empty their names into the Rio Grande. West of here the San Juans, east and north the Sangre de Cristos. Deep canyons of spruce, pine and aspen, million dollar homes built on the land that used to be ours. One person was even vain enough to have the logs for his home shipped here from Germany. Apparently this is somewhat of a feat. We should be in awe of his wealth, of his home he no longer likes and now wants to sell for $600,000. I resent this man, his wealth, the others like him.

My neighbor to the east has a roof that wants to fly away. My neighbor to the north has yard sales where he sells his furniture and, on one occasion, a single tire complete with rim. What invisible thing might lead a person to sell one lonesome tire? I love that tire and the dim hope it represents.

People send their kids to other schools. I resent them too. People quit on their community. For them, because I think survival is not quitting, I offer my resentment. Resentment as social capital. Yes. Today, we are made rich by just such a gift.

Let me explain the gift of resentment. In the absence of money, of employment opportunities, of culture and language effaced by assimilation and poverty, in this void there is room for little else. For me resentment is something synonymous with the aforementioned survival. Many might equate it with anger, and while that has its place, anger is, too often, destructive. Anger is the fire burning out of control. Resentment is the slow work of erosion, an erosion that cuts away at the pain of memory and loss. Resentment is water frozen in stone, the lick of wind that bends trees in supplication, the glacier whose blue heart cuts the world into being. Resentment is the long and arduous work that shapes people into something more beautiful. Because I resent the people who send their children to other schools I will carve my school into something better. I will not, in a fit of anger, burn away my school for another because the grass will come up, temporarily, greener. In short, wealth, like anger, is transitory, fleeting, brief, ephemeral. Things like language, culture and history, even these things, all of them beautiful, can be disappeared. I argue that if you resent these losses you will not let your town, your children, your culture, your language, your beauty disappear.

To me social capital is something that replenishes itself, a deep well that does not recede. My town is beautiful. In some ways my town is the fallen Hector. My town, most of it, is poor. My town and its people are those birds that do not leave as winter approaches.

These birds perch themselves on the razors of ice that hover just above the river and perhaps they resent the cold and snow, resent too the short and bleak days, the other birds that flew away. What could there possibly be for those heart-sized birds to eat, how do they keep, what gift sustains them through a January night? It can only be one thing, the unspendable gift their body holds, the drum thump of the heart that is survival, and is therefore a gift.

Be well my friend.

a.

An Open Letter Upon Seeing the Stars In A New Way

He was tall and rocked back and forth when he drove. i know little of him, great grandfather, Juan Sanchez. i know he could irrigate and farm better than any man in Mogote, perhaps better than any man in the valley. i know him because of the stories. He showed up one day at my parent's home; my mom and dad had just married. They had nothing, really, to show for their new marriage. This is the story i heard. My grandpa John shows up at the door one day. There is no mention of what he was driving or if he rocked back and forth the entire way to Denver. He comes to the door with grandma Becky. They plan on staying. My parents have very little but they welcome them, the travelers from el valle de san luis who had come north. Here is how my parents got their first t.v. Juan and Rebecca charged it to their Wards card, and that is how it happened. This in itself is not such a great story; i know this. But the way Juan has come to me ever since is the way the story should work itself out.

They are always together my great grandpa John and grandma Becky. i never knew him, but my grandma i knew until i was in my teens. She slept most often, already old, tired, in the back room of her daughter's house, my abuelita's. But there were days, often when it was cold and nobody wished to be outside, when she would rise from her bed of springs and lumps with its many many blankets. She would rise and begin walking toward the front door. She would walk east, almost instinctively. Sometimes she would make it quite far, other times we caught her on the dirt road just outside the house. We would ask her *"grandma where are you going?"* "home" she would reply *"pa mi casa."* What innate star directed her i will never know, what sense of judgment pointed her in the right direction, toward a house twenty years abandoned. *"Juan me esta esperando."* she would say. He had died in 1962 of a heart that no longer worked. We told her once that he had died "many years ago" we said. She did not know how to react, but could only remember him living, farming, strong. That was the last time we told her that he had died. We didn't want to see her scared in all her wrinkles, weak in her thin legs which moved in short steps. Later we would tell her "*grandpa will be here soon.*" She would wait with her memories and eventually fall asleep for days at a time.

So now i am a writer. Michele and i have moved back to the valley from what seemed like a long way away. i thought of Juan Sanchez while i was away, but he is stronger here, in the fields i cut for my brother and father. He is strongest in the mornings on the empty roads filled with pot-holes. It is here that i remember that he died in 1962. Can you miss a man you never knew? Did i really ever leave this place? Or, did i wait patiently like my grandma Becky for the place to come to me. My patience fulfilled in a way hers never quite was.

i thought of both of them my first night back. Saw their skinny figures in the stars, the grass that grew high this year. i had always wanted to return to my home, like my grandma Becky on those winter mornings opening the chain link gate, shuffling east in her bathrobe and thick slippers, her white hair in a braid. Moving in the direction the compass cannot define, home.

i think of Juan and Rebecca showing up at a door one day, to stay. The t.v. they charged was not important, but then again it was just that. "*Here's a t.v.*" they must have said. Here's a story you can tell your youngest, the one who will never know me, but will remember my generosity. So it is, here on this empty road lined by fields thick with hay.

To Whom It May Concern (Cami I):

Today, a Sunday, I wake to a fresh snow and a sky blank as chalk. These two things, seemingly irrelevant, do not discount the fact that I have hardly slept for the thought of my cousin Cami and the task of writing this letter have not left me for days now. If I'm being honest, I've needed to write this letter for over two years, ever since the last time I saw my cousin. She was still beautiful, friendly as ever, but it was obvious to those of us that know and knew her that something had faded from the deep well of her eyes and skin, the place where life resides for the outside world to recognize and comment on. My cousin, she of the blue sky and perpetual smile was now this chalky ghost of the person I used to know.

Again, if I'm being honest, I don't know exactly what she has gotten into. Obviously there have been drugs, run-ins with the law, numerous trips before the bench and, regrettably, jail. But there is more than this, some deeper pit of despair that I or a majority of her family cannot know. A little over two years ago, the last time I saw Cami, she had begun her descent into this unknowable place and those of us that know her were left to remember her as the Cami we used to know, the girl who could sit a horse better than any man, the young woman always at the ready with a hug or smile, my first cousin made of denim, pearl snaps, and white Stetson, racing her horse onto the rodeo grounds, her and her animal one being, as she waved up to the stands where her family sat. I remember my grandma Beatrice; she would only leave her house once a month, usually for groceries and to pick up her Social Security check. I remember her, even today, nearly 20 years after her death, as this balance of frugality and uncharted affection for living things. She sat to my right, three seats over, and her smile, sometimes as rare as an eclipse, spread across her face as Cami came toward us, waving with her left hand, hard and fast from the elbow, her fingers pressed tight against her thumb; she was slicing away at the air, my grandma smiled, and all of us were happy.

It comes to this. When I think of Cami I have always thought of life and happiness, and it pains me now to think that her life, that of so much promise and even more love, could become this broken thing sent away to prison as if that promise and love were not something worth redemption. I argue that they are.

Earlier, I mentioned the blank and chalky sky and alluded to the fact that it is Sunday. There is no small coincidence in this detail. For it was a single thought that kept me up most of the night, a scripture from the Gospel of Luke, where the shepherd leaves his flock of 99 to seek out the one sheep that has strayed off into the wilderness.

Cami grew up on a ranch and both of her parents did the same. I do not tell you this for the obvious reasons, those of hard work, responsibility and more hard work. I tell you this because her mother's side of the family, to this day, run sheep. That too, in and of itself, is no great thing, but it reminds me of the scripture alluded to earlier. It was Jesus who told of the shepherd who went off in search of that lost sheep, and it was the finding of that sheep that always struck me as disingenuous, bordering on the false. I know, too well, the experience of seeking out the lost sheep and their finding. It is always an inconvenience, always too much trouble, the lost sheep hemmed back into the flock with cursing, thrown stones and the brute voice of admonishment, the lost sheep always beyond the edge of our control, running this way and then the other, a lightning bolt of fear and confusion, sometimes finding its way back to the others, but too often running in the exact opposite direction than the one intended. So it struck me as odd that the shepherd did not curse or chase the lost sheep back into the fold. Instead, he placed the lost animal upon his shoulders and carried it back to its rightful place.

From what I understand of the situation, the courts and Cami's family have tried to hem Cami back into the person she was by use of threats, punishment and tough love, and true to life, the intended course of such urging has not been followed. What Cami needs, in my estimation, is a herder to carry her back to the 99 who were not lost. Prison, alone, is not the answer. I am not saying that Cami has not broken the law, nor am I saying that she deserves to get off the hook entirely. What she does need, however, is mercy. The parable of the lost sheep, the one quoted here, is from Luke.

Luke 15: 3-6

> [3] Then Jesus told them this parable: [4] "Suppose one of you has a hundred sheep and loses one of them. Does he not leave the ninety-nine in the open country and go after the lost sheep until he finds it? [5] And when he finds it, he joyfully puts it on his shoulders [6] and goes home. Then he calls his friends and neighbors together and says, 'Rejoice with me; I have found my lost sheep.'

In the other gospels, quite often, when they refer to Jesus' love they use the word "perfect," but Luke, the physician, the healer, must have known that humans, all of us, are flawed, wounded by our ailments and our failings; Luke, when he refers to Jesus' love uses the word "merciful." It was only in Luke's version that Jesus forgave the sinner crucified next to him, the thief Dismas. I ask sincerely and humbly, that the courts show some measure of mercy when sentencing my cousin. Her life is worth saving. I ask, on behalf of my family and hers, that this court put away its handful of stones and instead offer Cami the rehabilitation she so obviously needs.

It has come this point . . . quite literally in my opinion, where there is a life in the balance, teetering at the ledge of one pit on the abyss of another. I ask that your honor offer a hand up, that you temper justice with mercy and bring Cami back to us so that we may be, once again, happy, once again, a family.

Sincerely,

Aaron A. Abeyta

A Letter to the Graduating Class of 2008, Coronado High School, Gallina, New Mexico

Dear Graduates,

Antonito Colorado is a small blip of a town, barely perceptible on the radar of people passing through. They sometimes see the broken windows, the gutted and lonely buildings, invariably there will be a any number of lost souls, sometimes swimming in an ocean of alcohol and distant memory. This is where I am from, a place where it always seems to be windy, where other people from other towns look down upon us. Sometimes I'm asked,

"Where are you from?"

"Antonito" I say.

"I'm sorry," they respond.

Other times I'm asked the same question, a question of my origins, and I tell them, and the response comes back.

"No, before that."

I guess they want me to admit that my ancestors haven't been here for centuries. They want for me to admit that their image of my town is the same as their image of me. As though I have nothing to offer the world, simply because I am from a place that is poor, a town that is small and a school that is even smaller. I don't know if these same things happen to the residents of Gallina and the graduates of Coronado High School, but I guess that ignorance does not exist solely on Highway 285 as it drives through my hometown. I want this letter to be against ignorance, I want it to be a marker for how you live your life beyond the walls of this school. I want for each of you to be happy, to do great things, to become the person you've always envisioned.

I'm sure that each of you has heard, in some context or another, that happiness is best when it is shared. You need look no further than your family gatherings for an example of how this is true. Simply put, your happiness is linked to this place, and whether you believe it or not, so is your success. What people on straight highways don't realize is that a community like this one is a great circle, and what they really don't realize is that for humans it is the circle that sustains us. Wherever you go, and whatever good you do in the world, I have a simple request. Remember that no fruit is possible without the roots. Always give credit to your school and your community. Always give credit to the place where your ancestors dreamt you into existence, give credit to the place where they are buried, where their spirit lives like memory, like water, like everything that sustains you, give credit to your parents, your family, your friends, your teachers, give credit to the place where you first realized what you could make of your life.

It is the place we're from that provides the place from which we're judged, and that is your challenge. Make your hometown, your school, your own family better.

It is easy enough to say that you are from somewhere; it is more difficult to actually be from somewhere, to contribute to a place is a sacrifice. Please don't think of sacrifice as something negative. Of all the gifts your parents ever gave you the ones you will remember are the ones they sacrificed for so that you could have something better. Every sacrifice is inherently blessed because it gives of itself so that others can prosper. You must give of yourself to make things better. Change cannot exist in a vacuum, nor can goodness. You must become the change you wish to see in the world. You must sacrifice many long hours at school, at your job in order to taste the sweet fruit of the tree. If you are lucky enough to taste of the sweet fruit of whatever success means to you, please know that sharing it makes it even sweeter. This, more than anything is what your community knows. We are no longer a culture like we used to be, willing to share everything for the betterment of the whole. Yet the values of that not so distant culture still exist within us. We are still, despite being burned, being marginalized, and sometimes forgotten, we are still a generous people whose first instinct is to share what is good about us. Don't let the world take that away from you. Don't let the shiny things that society says you need become what sustains you. Everything you will ever need to survive in this or any world comes from this place, your hometown. Trust me on this. Always find it within yourself to share and allow that sharing to benefit your community.

When it comes to my hometown there are plenty of problems. Even though the same powerful and benevolent circles that exist here exist in Antonito, there are other equally powerful circles that do their best to undermine the integrity of a community and its people. Often these circles are referred to as cycles, and with your energy, intelligence, youth and willpower certain cycles can be broken. I hope that your willingness to sacrifice and return to your community also has the added effect of breaking the negative cycles that too often consume us. For example, my hometown is plagued by the cycles of poverty, land loss, alcoholism, complacency and the worst of all the cycles, fear. Too often, especially when someone says or does something against us, we are hesitant to act, to educate the ignorant, to change or interrupt the cycle which diminishes us. For some reason our instinct, in the face of adversity and displeasure, is to run away or remain silent. I pray that each of you has, as a requisite for life, courage to stand up against any force that tries to break the circles your ancestors and community have sought, for centuries, to form. If anything, I want this letter to serve as a reminder to always stand up for what you know is right. Do not allow others to judge you or diminish you. Be strong in your knowledge and your abilities. Be strong so that your community can also be strong. Be strong so that your circle may grow and become more powerful. Always dream in circles, always be willing to sacrifice for others, always be ready and able to stand up against ignorance, wherever you encounter it.

In closing, I want to wish each of you the very best and extend my sincere appreciation for being allowed to speak to you on this important day, I pray that your youth and energy serve you well and I pray that they someday serve the world and this community well. May every place be made better by your entering it and may your former places be made better by your having been there.

God Bless and good luck.

A Letter to an Adopted Son

Dear Marcos,

We have both made that trip into the valle; so i know you will understand. The long straight road from Pueblo to Walsenburg, where you think you will travel into the heart of the Spanish Peaks. They rise like two breasts left there to suckle the universe, their milk flowing in two directions. One goes back to our mother, through the desert of Sonora, through the railhead at Celaya, back in time to her womb of water on Tezcoco. She is standing knee deep. Her bare brown feet have gathered mud between the toes. She is from two worlds, like you.

Marcos, you are the milk which flows in two directions, and you are not sure which way to flow. South toward the valle looking for a mother who gave birth to you in a town named after cottonwoods, or south further still to a woman standing knee deep in Tezcoco. So you shuffle through papers of year in which the water kept no record. So that when you stand knee deep in the Conejos you will look at home, the water turning in slow green ripples around your legs, the soft line from your pole searching the bottom of the river for a piece of your history.

i watch as you read the scales of a fish as though they were maps to somewhere else. The red streak on the fish's belly tells you that she is spawning, that within her belly there are orange eggs which she will lay beneath a rock, and that they will hatch without knowing their mother. You hold her, this mother, in your hand; you feel the turning of her spine as she slips from your hand into the green water. i know now, why you let her go.

Cover Letter

Dear Rut,

  i am writing to apply for the recently posted position as your father with a specialization in fly fishing, coaching, and other skills not usually associated with being the father of a young girl. My considerable investigations have contributed greatly to my dissertation titled *The intricate workings of fate in a modern world: the several coincidences of being human on this mortal coil.* Through the course of my research i have determined that you are originally from Addis Ababa, where presumably you lived on the streets with a mother who loved you enough to give you up. My studies have been versed in irony at times, but this particular irony will be the well-source of my continued academic investigation.

  My ongoing research examines my life up to this point, how sometimes i feel this void, some might call it a chasm formed by grief, unanswered prayers and a frozen grave i dug one January afternoon. i believe this research contributes greatly to my ongoing literary, rhetorical, anthropological and pedagogical discourse. i am fluent in two languages and sometimes dabble in the many varied ways of saying hello in languages outside of my current fluency contexts, take, for example, selam, in what i imagine to be your native language.

  i have considerable experience discerning the connections between early loss and modern acceptance as a historical mode of figuration, and i believe that my academic record is such that you can be assured of the following: i will love you and look after you, promising such things as a dance on your wedding night (God Willing), to defend you against teachers who find your obvious brilliance to be an affront or challenge to their authority. In a similar vein, i know that other children can be mean; they will comment on the magnificence of your hair in a way that is not kind, yet i believe that my considerable training and acumen in such matters, honed on football players, nieces, nephews and a spattering of bullies present in my own life, have left me more than equipped to handle the responsibilities of defending your young spirit while continuously nurturing your ongoing thirst for discovery and knowledge.

i have worked on what some of my colleagues have deemed the mythological structures of early to contemporary 21st century societies; perhaps you recognize these constructs as a devotion to La Virgen Madre de Dios, known as Mari to you. This phenomena is also evidenced by the deep reverent bows you make in front of the altar, the motioning of your tiny tiny hand encouraging us to get closer to the baptism, as if it were possible to more readily see the holy spirit entering into the child's body and life. In short, the inter-continental influence of faith has made a similar entrance into my life as it has yours.

My most recent publications are exercises in persistence and perseverance, two traits that make for sad poems, but have allowed me to pursue the many facets of what being a father would entail. It is my hope that these various works will manifest themselves in texts which examine connections which are significant despite the inordinate distance between Ethiopia and Antonito. In addition, my studies will look into the considerable miracle of what certain scholars and laymen dub the wheel of fate that brought a child, such as yourself, into my life without any obvious design, other than the one sketched for us as some arrangement we all, somehow, invisibly follow.

In terms of my most rewarding teaching experiences i believe that those are yet to come, though i did find significant satisfaction teaching courses on literature and culture where my classes demanded diverse racialized and gendered ways of reading. For instance, i am a man and you are still just a girl, and i am a chicano and you are an Ethiopian Coptic Catholic by birth; yet we are, in a most mutually beneficial way, thrown here together. And i cannot help but think of rows of canola joined in the hottest month by bees that shuttle back and forth, back and forth, ferried so by wishes their worker hearts and bombus terrestris pollen baskets undoubtedly carry from yellow flower, to yellow flower, to yellow flower, to yellow flower and so on, forever without cease, so that in some theoretical paradigm there might be honey, in both a literal and figurative sense, where the latter is a life where i might be able to fulfill my duties as your father while still being solidly grounded in the academic world that will, someday, come in handy as you labor over the proper use of a comma or semicolon.

As you consider my application, it must be noted that my spouse and love of my life is also a diligent and thoughtful academician whose scholarly goals coincide with mine but have a flair all their own. We are hoping for an opportunity to team teach in a co-curricular setting where both of our many parental attributes can be most effectively realized. Her skills include but are not limited to the remarkable ability to make people stop crying and an uncanny way of marking the measure of a person after only a brief interaction with them. Therefore, it would be a considerable investment on your part to heed her advice, as i have never known her to be wrong about the soul nor the intent of another human being. For instance, she loved you immediately and thinks of you constantly.

While i realize that there may be many other qualified candidates, some of which may have more publications as well as hands-on pedagogical and institutional training, i assure you that none of them will work as hard as yours truly. While this may be viewed as arrogant to some, i believe that humility is rarely rewarded in the spirit with which it was expressed. Put another way, the humble person is often overlooked in favor of a more "qualified" and bombastic candidate that is ill-equipped to handle the intricacies and subtle beauty that a quiet child brings to a relationship. i offer that i am both capable of silence or vigor depending on the context of any particular moment; i am adaptable, diligent, and accountable. i look forward to further interaction with you in the very near future. i pray, that i am afforded the opportunity to work with you and for you. i assure you that my candidacy is legitimate and my intent is to make a lifelong commitment to you, your upbringing and the starry luminosity of your spirit which i find so mesmerizing and exciting, the very same pure illumination that is also my resolve, a resolve which is only diminished by the greater light that is your smile.

sincerely,
aaron a. abeyta

A Letter, Of Sorts, To My Agapetos Somatiko Eidei

Dear Agapetos,

I write this to you
I write this letter of love to you
I write this to you, you of eyes laden with sleep
You of the sunken face
You of the hands made of stone and grit
You of the several horses in the field
You of the wisdom that even the devil knows God exists
You of the cottonwoods along the rivers edge
You of the knowledge that forgiveness is part and parcel of our faith
Antonito of the poor
Antonito of the rich in spirit
Antonito of Spanish voices
My Antonito of too many funerals
You of the broken window
You of the Blackbirds in winter
You of the Robins in spring
You of the loud trucks on mainstreet
Antonito of three rivers
Antonito of two bars, two liquor stores, and one library
You of my mother's prayers
You of the burning candle
You of the presence of God in the altar
You of a broken and humbled heart
You of the Lord will not scorn
You of the rolled back stone
Antonito of a Swallow's mud nest in summer
Antonito of wind
Antonito of loss
Antonito of abundant grace

You of Hail Marys
You of ice
You of snow that melts to mud
You of the cow that returns to where her calf last nursed
You of a single child on a swing
You of a single drunk on a corner
You of divinity
You of sin
My Antonito of hawks on thermals
You my hometown of ducks on the Conejos
Antonito of headgates and shovels
You of broken dreams
You of sheep spreading themselves on a mountainside
You of abuelitas baking bread
You of the untie him and let him go
You of grain scattered from a human hand
Antonito of timber and roads of gravel
Antonito of bugling elk
You, my place, of antelope like ghosts
You this town of poets
You this single guitar
You this flute of prayer
Antonito of men who drink wood alcohol
Antonito of men who throw rocks
Antonito of men who die behind gas stations
You of men who caress the faces of infants
You my town of outsiders
You my town of people come to save us
Antonito, you, my town, that has already been saved
You of penitente crosses on mesas
You of barefoot ghosts

You of brothers that bleed at the fists of the other
You of ten lepers healed
You of one leper that says thank you
You, my town, of losing lottery tickets
You, my town, of missed free throws
My agapetos of men with stained hats
My agapetos of women who outlive their men
You of the Samaritan woman at the well
You of the man blind from birth
You of Lazarus
You of spy Tuesday
You of 39 scourges at the pillar
You of water that flows east
You of trout in the deepest holes
You of fences
You of no trespassing
You, my town, of moonlight on llano
My Antonito of yellow butterflies dancing at the edges of puddles
You of the machinery in the fields
Antonito of rows of cut hay
Antonito of 2:00 a.m. semis heading south
Antonito of volcanic rock
Antonito of stone hearts
Antonito of forgiveness
You, my hometown, of perfect spirals
You, my hometown, of rumor
You, my hometown, of a coyote hunting mice in a meadow
You of the fact that Jesus was sold for the price of a slave
You of 30 pieces of silver
You of ditch water spilling
You of ditches sold dry

Antonito of fishermen

Antonito of extinction

Antonito of mestizos

Antonito of indios who wish themselves spanish

Antonito of indios that do not wish themselves spanish

My agapetos of a kiss on the cheek

My hometown of several losses and a single victory

You of railroads

You of perlite

You of devoured mountains

You of second homes

You of canyons

You of Ravens in pairs at the highway's edge

You of cold well water

You of Good Friday

My agapetos of broken things

My hometown of wedding marches

You of silent books

You of wood chopped and piled

You of holding hands

You of Matanzas

You of sacrifice

You of redemption

My agapetos of villages of memory

My hometown of a white horse that carries the dead

You of Canon

You of San Antonio

You of Track City

You of Ortiz

You of Los Pinos

You of La Isla

You of La Florida
You of Las Mesitas
You of Fox Creek
You of Mogote
You of Lobatos
You of Guadalupe
You of Conejos
You of San Miguel
You of Santa Rita
Antonito of tin roofs
Antonito of stained glass
Antonito of adobe
You, my hometown, of orange tarps in spring
Agapetos of onion in a skillet
Agapetos of red chile
Agapetos of tortillas made from scratch
Agapetos of female hands
Agapetos of skin like bible pages
You of thin and beautiful things
You of chamizo
You of falling sprinkler water
You of potatoes in bloom
You of ancient grudges
You of silence and stares
You of other schools
You of red
Antonito of alfalfa
Antonito of purple
Antonito of palms as symbols of heroes
Antonito of Barabas as us
Antonito of I Thirst

Antonito of they offered him a sponge soaked in vinegar
Agapetos of white and gold
Antonito of my youth
Antonito of my day
You of good boots
You of cruising mainstreet
You of letters left unread
You of the memory of picking peas
You of dams built
You of fires in January
You of pinon smoke
Antonito of forgotten things
Hometown of women in prayer
Hometown of jump shots
Hometown of line drives
Hometown of fastballs and curves
You, my agapetos, of minds lost to drugs
Agapetos of churches and signs of a Blessed Mother
You of confession
You of admission
You of Rosary beads
You of things human
You of myth
You of weeping
You of ache
You of piled stone
My hometown of sky
Antonito of clear days
Antonito of spruce
Antonito of shadows longest at dusk
Antonito of dust

Antonito of life as penultimate
Antonito of catalogs that give us back our names
Antonito of Cuaresma y Pascua
You of this place without end
You of this place where we all begin
You of this place where joy is born
You hometown
You agapetos
You
Yes you
You agapetos somatiko eidei

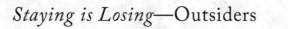

Staying is Losing—Outsiders

A Letter to the Headwaters from the Sovereign Banks of the Conejos

Dear George,

It is good to be writing again. The mountains have snow. The air is cold. The sun is shining. It is a good November day and i have been thinking of you and this idea of sovereignty, an almost foreign word here where there is so much poverty and most of us, to some degree, rely on a government, that mostly ignores us, to survive. i suppose the skeptic in me believes that the government wants its minorities that way, dependent, but i don't want this letter to be about bitterness. Instead, i want you to come to the river with me where we can talk about this beautiful wish, sovereignty. Both words, river and sovereignty, lead me to Gerald Arellano.

i looked up sovereignty in the dictionary. i was hoping for something that didn't mention autonomy, politics or governance. i was hoping because in terms of those words, Antonito does not necessarily fit. In any of those arenas were are not heavy hitters. However, as of late, i've found that the dictionary is a place for discovery. i held out hope and there it was. The first definition. Before autonomy. Before body politic. There waiting for us on page 836 of my Webster's Seventh New Collegiate was this definition. "Supreme excellence or an example of it." It made reference to Shakespeare's *Love's Labour's Lost*, "*of all the complexions the cull'd sovereignty do meet in her fair cheek.*"

So with this i come to Gerald Arellano who has been haunting my poetry for years now. Growing up in Canon, he was our nearest neighbor, about ¼ mile away to the east. For most people, Gerald would not come to mind as an example of supreme excellence. As men go, he had the basic features of a man but did not exude any other characteristics we think of when we say the word 'man.' He was a thin man, almost non-existent, his tall brown body racked with diabetes, alcoholism, drug abuse. He lived in an un-insulated trailer with his wife and daughter. Later these two would die in the most horrible traffic accident i have ever seen. Gerald asked that i be one of the six that carried his daughter to her grave, but the tragedy of

Gerald Arellano existed long before his family was taken from him. He did not work. Their home had no running water, and to survive he waited for his welfare check. In his daily life he was not an example of supreme excellence.

Usually around Christmas, my abuelito would hire Gerald to do some work around the ranch. Just some under the radar stuff paid in cash every weekend. We knew he wouldn't return after the first payday. We hired him anyway because my abuelito liked Gerald's father. i tell you all this because in the eyes of this nation and our community Gerald Arellano was close to worthless. Yet, as a boy i admired him more than any other man i knew. i believe in my God; i see him as loving, a presence, who despite the traumas of our lives, gives each of us a gift. A gift of supreme excellence.

This conference deals with the headwaters of many great rivers and communities. One river, the Conejos which drops toward the Rio Grande, has a special place in my heart. It was on this river that i learned about supreme excellence. His name was Gerald Arellano. He died of his failings a few years back. He probably wasn't over forty years old. i failed to record the day, month and year of his passing, but this letter will serve to record that he was the greatest fisherman i have ever known.

As a young boy i would look east out of our living room window and wait for his thin ghostlike figure to emerge from his weathered, white, trailer, rod in hand and move slowly north toward the river.

i had a dream about Gerald the other day. i had walked into a room where sadness was tangible, a thick humidity of despair. My dream saw Gerald and many others like him, and my dream told me to seek out their beauty. The dream asked me to save them with their own gift by using mine, these words.

And so i would wait for him to move north toward the river and i would run to stand by his side, my own fishing pole ready to mimic his cast, the holes, the retrieval of the lure. i was his mirror. Everyone thought he was a bum, but he would catch 20, 30 fish. i would beg some from him to make four, enough for my mother, father, brother and myself. He always shared.

So what does any of this have to do with the sovereignty? As a writer i must have faith that one human can represent all of us. Gerald Arellano is that for me. By all accounts he had nothing, and what little he had was taken from him at an intersection two miles up the road from his trailer. Antonito, while she still has more than Gerald, has had many things taken from her. Some are measurable as in acres and cubic feet of water. Other losses are more discreet but just as devastating. To be sovereign, autonomous, self-governing, economically viable, free, each of us must realize our one gift. Sometimes, if God and genetics are good there are many to choose from, but often there is just that one, the one that cannot be stolen because people don't look into the well past the water they have come to drink. Each of us, each community despite circumstance or poverty, must foster the one gift, the one resource, our one example of supreme excellence. If we do this, sovereignty becomes easier. Some may argue that setting the gift free opens it up to be stolen. i stood by Gerald's side, mimicked him to the smallest detail, used the same lures and equipment and still, twenty years later, i cannot match him.

Many have suggested that gambling will save Antonito. We have had enough of the odds. Some have compared Antonito to other communities, detailed how we might also benefit from outside enterprise, whether it be private prisons, ski slopes or cabins in a formerly pristine canyon; i believe that only our gift can save us, not what someone else says is the cure. To be sovereign we must realize our natural gifts and harvest them. We cannot be complacent or happy with the scraps of the American dream. We must let our excellence be our mark.

Perhaps Gerald Arellano was a bum. He was beautiful too, excellent, supremely so, there on the Conejos where this boy and maybe even the fish miss him. On the Conejos he was free, autonomous, memorable, totally aware that some gifts cannot be purchased, stolen, neglected or lost. Years later, i too realize something, only the beautiful parts of our existence can save us.

George, here's hoping that salvation of this sort finds each of us.

Your friend,

a.

47

A Letter from the Confluence of a Very Old River, Ghosts, and a Few Brief Moments of Light

Yes, all of this is sorrow. But leave
a little love burning always
like the small bulb in the room of a sleeping baby
that gives him a bit of security and quiet love
though he doesn't know what the light is
or where it comes from.

—*Yehuda Amichai*

Yes, all of this is sorrow. I struggle to tell my brain—be positive damn it, before the entire world begins to think that you live in the saddest place in the universe—tell them how your people have survived for generations, their lives held together by an ancient dialect of Spanish, Nahual, English and even a small teaspoon of French here and there. Tell them how your abuelita would fry you an egg on winter mornings, how the puela would pop and sizzle while your young heart filled with how much you loved her. I want to tell you all of these things, but, alas, I cannot.

In the pre-dawn we see the ghosts as they move up and down Main Street, malnourished doppelgangers intent on their morning bottle. There is no buoyancy in their stride, in their lives. Their failures and their pain were predicted before they were born. We can spot them, the oncoming brokenness of being that is my gente; we have become the weather men of damaged things, able to spot the low pressure fronts above the San Juans, the shifting jet stream of prosperity, the storm that is forming off the coast of some distant place over some ocean that most of these ghosts will never see. We name their thin and frail bodies so that our children will know them, so that they may avoid the gravity that holds them in their orbit of failure.

Look mijo, that one is a waste of God-given talent.

That one is a bum.

That one, mijo, he could shoot the basketball, but his name is acid now, drugs mijo, the acid fried his brain.

And that one, the one on the corner his legs bowed like a harp placed in front of a mirror, that one was beaten with a bat.

And that one, his father never loved him.

And that one over there is just like his father. Yes mijo sometimes prison is hereditary.

And that one, your classmate, try and be nice to him, his mother was driving home one night, the pass was so icy. I'm going to tell you something mijo, our secret, please do not tell your friends; they will just make fun of him. When he drinks, which is always, he takes his mother's high school ID out of his wallet and he stares at it. Be nice to that one mijo, I don't know why God has done that to him.

And so we name and continue to name them, their stories are our warning, and here is a small truth that makes this letter nearly impossible; I have only named a few of our ghosts.

The ghosts are so visible, there on the main drag. They have been there so long we cannot know if the gutted buildings they lean up against need their thin bodies to remain standing or if the reciprocal is true. People drive through and they make the easy assumption that everyone makes when looking at broken and abandoned things. This place is poor. The assumption itself is not incorrect, but I'm going to offer that the assumption is so rarely benign or born of winged things that might make a positive difference. Poverty has always been the excuse for exploitation, the knife sharpened against the benevolent idea that help is being offered.

At the south end of town there are black railcars, black gondolas, which wait on the tracks like tumors, patient as only nuclear gondolas can be, their hollowed bellies waiting for the cargo of nuclear waste from Los Alamos National Laboratories. To the north of the black gondolas the Rio San Antonio flowers over an ancient skull of volcanic rock, and I imagine that the rock remembers its fiery birth, holds it, cool now, a heart of pain that keeps the river flowing.

There are so many ghosts we keep alive, all of them are passed down to us, hereditary markers where we store pain, loss, humiliation along with the small crumb of love we keep in our vast heart of ache and longing. Our resilience is our pain. Our land was stolen and then our water. Our language was next. A young boy, sincerely asks me what I think of the black rail cars. I tell him that I expected them all along. I mean this. Most everyone believes that they just arrived one day; they did appear without an announced warning, but we have all been instructed by our loss.

"Mijo, remember how they stole our water. It will become their habit."

So I tell the boy, they already took the land and water, now they are coming for our health. This is the story of conquest; every genocide has its rail cars.

I cannot shake this image. I see it, permanent as memory will allow. Primo Levi called her the Hiroshima Schoolgirl. She was one of the 150,000 vaporized, her shadow burned permanently into a wall. I search the internet and find images of other shadows, a man who was waiting for a bank to open, the shadow of leaves, the shadows of hand-rails, but I cannot find the girl's shadow.

Los Alamos calls it "legacy waste." This is their way of saying that the Uranium, PCB's and Radon are the byproduct of a heroic endeavor that ended the Second World War. They make it a point in the public meetings to tell us of its origins. You see the implication; it is our duty as patriots is to accept what the Department of Energy sends us because this waste, this legacy waste, saved American lives. I want to remind them that more Americans died in Hiroshima and Nagasaki than in the attacks of 9/11, a futile rebuttal to their jingoistic rhetoric.

Marie Max is from Cameron, Arizona; she is Navajo, and she tells us how the elementary school has water fountains wrapped in cellophane, the water too dangerous to drink, the government mined uranium has leached into the water supply. I think of Marie often; she says I remind her of a Navajo; it is one of the finest compliments I have ever received. She gives me an eagle feather after I read poetry to her. She doesn't explain why; I gladly accept. I think of Marie for many reasons. I remember the story of how she refused the bread brought to our table at Outback Steakhouse. She made the woman take it back and bring her a loaf that didn't have the knife sticking out of it. Her point was simple. Why would you stab your food? I don't know why I am telling you this. It must make sense, somewhere, somehow.

The gondolas wait for their cargo 250 feet from the San Antonio River; any accident or spill would, within minutes if not seconds, end up in the river, the town's water supply, the lifeblood of the acequias east of town, the water that blooms our fields, waters our animals and makes us whole.

Those ghosts, the ones I spoke of earlier. They have begun to write. They are finally asking to be heard. The town park is filled with their tags and graffiti. They announce their life in black paint. They claim this sad acre of park, where children rarely play, as their own. I believe in symbols, they have killed the park, the empty swings, the tagged slide. Their anger is palpable. Their abandonment has been complete for generations. So what is my point? Honestly, I'm not sure. I know this is all supposed to be connected. That is a writer's job, to connect what the heart knows to what the eyes see. These connections, these too are resilience, I suppose.

Energy Solutions and the railroad tell us the waste shipments will bring economic viability to Antonito. They want to ship the waste in perpetuity. That's a fancy word for forever, but we knew that before they opened their mouths. They see our ghosts, our beaten park, the worn sidewalks of despair. They see how we take every failure, cut it open, weigh and measure the vital organs, always looking for the source, the failed engine that caused the living host to succumb to his aching life and thus conquer it by dying. They see these things and therefore view our poverty as weakness. They see our fallen things and imagine it must mean complacency and apathy. Put a different way, they believe we won't fight back.

Gerald Vizenor coined a term, Survivance. The root is simple, survive. It's almost an equation, survival + resistance = living. Or survival + perseverance, or sustenance, or defiance, or assistance, or appearance, or circumstance. Perhaps it is survival + resilience. I know the suffix does not quite fit, but I think the gesture is accurate, the intent is pure enough to make it true. I mentioned earlier that our resilience is our pain, but I have written myself out of that assumption, though I may come back to it someday. Instead, I see now how our survival is our resilience. We will never bounce back to our original form as the definition of the word implies. Those days are gone, absent as a brief push of wind, here then gone. No, I suppose our survival and therefore our resilience will depend entirely on how long we wish to fight.

And what of those ghosts, those walking frailties of bone and poverty? I think of Marie Max, her refusal of the stabbed bread. I think of the town park overrun with graffiti and broken bottles. A question emerges, why?

225,000 people died in Hiroshima and Nagasaki. Their deaths were dropped on them with a parachute tethered to an atomic bomb. Their deaths were the result of genius minds working at evil intent. Antonito is in Colorado, but we are, culturally, linguistically, religiously, spiritually and emotionally tied to the people and places of northern New Mexico. Those 225,000 lives disappeared in an instant of demon wind and heat, and I have heard how all the radiation entered into the sky, how the wind brought it across the Pacific.

I don't want to be too melodramatic here, but I think you can see where I'm going with this. There must have been souls on that wind too, souls looking for the source of their destruction. I'm not entirely naïve. I don't buy into a whole lot of hocus pocus, but I don't believe that northern New Mexico and southern Colorado are some of the poorest places in the country simply because they are isolated. Can you imagine the weight of 225,000 deaths, how heavily that weighs on even the potential for resilience?

I realize that this letter is getting long. Perhaps you are tired. I will not be long in finishing. But I thought I should tell you that all is not death and poverty. I want you to know that I love my hometown. There are brief and brilliant moments of light, the sun through a kitchen window, neighbors that always wave as they pass, a herd of sheep as they emerge from the trees into a meadow, a river that forgets the sins we have committed against it, the memory of my abuelita frying me an egg on a winter morning, two kids just barely in love, holding hands as they walk down main street, a football team that takes the field one autumn and brings hope where none had previously resided. Yes, there are great storehouses of beauty, each made manifest by some small gesture or action. I want you to know that the gondolas have not moved in over a year. We are resilient enough to fight. We are in a great struggle of will and determination versus millions and millions of dollars, but we know, despite our losses, despite our ghosts, that the river is our home, that the river makes our home possible, that the river in its many moods and flows is the truest metaphor, it teaches us how to be, and at its lowest, when she appears dry and weak, we know beneath the rock of volcanoes and distant pressures, that the river still flows, invisible, subterranean, toward a confluence of hope, a place where it emerges from the earth sweet and cold, perhaps flowing into a greater river which flows toward a greater river and so on, our own resiliency borne there upon the riffles and currents, our lives complete, our ghosts smiling up at the passing earth, as the river carries them.

Much peace,

a.

A Letter to the Headwaters About Remembering My Father in the Future,

Dear George,

Again I am relying on the night for inspiration. Sometime within the next 24 hours I must write this letter to you. Antonito is mostly quiet; even the dogs are silent. In the not so far away distance a single car guns its engine and the sound dopplers toward me. I walk down the empty street and look toward Mars burning red; I recall that the paper reported our planetary neighbor, on this particular night, will be closer to earth than it has been in 600 centuries. After tonight it will spin away from us and never again, in our lifetime, approach us with such fire and proximity.

In the quiet Antonito night I hear that single car, the sound of its tires on the gravel of some side street, but I am not thinking about the car or Mars any longer. My father has entered my thoughts. He has made himself the subject of this letter. My father, whose stubbornness and disdain for false authority I've inherited, rises in my mind in much the same way he always rises in the darkness before dawn, noisily but with purpose. He works harder than any person I know and years from now, after he and Mars have spun away from me, that is one of the things I will remember.

I will remember how he woke me at 4 a.m. so that I could begin the day's work. I will remember the winter of my sophomore year in high school when I was mother to 35 orphan lambs. I will remember how those lambs baaahhhed in the early cold of winter mornings as I walked toward them with warm bottles of milk. I will remember the stars and the way the moon was sometimes still in the sky. But mostly I will remember the night in early spring when a pack of dogs attacked my family of penco lambs. I will remember how seventeen of them died and seventeen more were left, in some way or another, covered in their own blood. In the midst of all that carnage there was one lamb left completely untouched. He was born blind and had learned to follow the other lambs by sound. I named him ciego, because he was, after all, blind. He had escaped the dogs because

54

he was the only lamb that did not run. In all the commotion he had lost contact with the other lambs and therefore stood blind and still as the others were, one by one, run down.

Years from now, when I remember my father in the future, I will think of that lamb, not for his blindness but because he did not run. My father will come to me in every season of my life and I will remember that he too never ran away. Some have accused my father of being a troublemaker, always demanding that the highest standards apply to his family, community and people. In his own way he demands perfection and many are threatened by his unwillingness to concede even the slightest bit of weakness. Others say that he is, in some figurative sense of the word, blind to the changing world, that if he chose to he could be debt free and not have to work so hard. All he would have to do for this version of the American Dream is sell his ranch and live off of the profits. People tell him he would be happy if he did this; they ask him to see better, to see how the ranch is the root of every misstep in his life.

My father tells this story of his youth and the two dreams he had for what he would become. The first was an FBI agent and the second was a rancher. I believe he counts himself among the luckiest of men to have attained at least one of his dreams. My father, in the future, will come to me in the bend of the river where it meets the meadow, in the thick and bent autumn barley, in the first trickle of ditch water in spring, his memory will surface and persist in the rising haystacks, the sheep spreading out along a hillside, he will rise in my memory like pale llano dust and I too will consider him lucky to have known and fought for one of his two dreams.

I do not think it is an accident that he is the only full-scale rancher in Antonito with a Hispanic surname. So much has gone away from Antonito, so much poverty where once there was ownership and prosperity. Amongst the fallen lambs of Antonito's past my father persists despite the Farmers Home Administration appraiser projecting his crop output as 1/3 less than his neighbor's when all that separates the two fields is a thin string of barbed wire and the thick canyon of a person's last name. I see him rise daily despite the same appraiser telling him that his land is worth $45,000 dollars less than smaller pieces just up the road from us. He knows in his persistent heart that this is so simply because those ranches are white owned. He knows in the memory of his heart that those same ranches were sold away by his own people, and he knows there is no happiness in their profit. I have seen my father endure when environmentalists destroyed the float on his stock tanks, allowing 30,000 gallons of water to flood over the trough and create a mud so thick that seven cows and seven calves lost their lives trying to pull themselves free of it. I have seen him fall to his knees and give a dying calf mouth to mouth. I have seen him drop to those same knees in a mud and manure filled corral and nurse a dying lamb from its mother's swollen ubre. I have seen him rise in the early light of so many mornings and drive to so many banks that I have lost count. My father, when I remember him in the future, will have persisted through winter storms that buried sheep alive, through the words of "educated" books that call him a recipient of ranch welfare. My father who persisted through a bank loan that insisted he have collateral for 115% of the loan's value will be, in my future memory of him, a man I would like to become, powerful and unafraid.

George, you asked me to write about the American Dream and I will be perfectly honest I don't know what that means. The dream we all hope for seems so multi-faceted and clichéd that I cannot reconcile it with the dreams I am familiar with, so singular and persistently real. I suppose I must understand the dreams of my father as the dreams of every person who sets foot in this country of ours. The American Dream should be free of arbitrary distinctions and labels that are pre-determined to represent worth. In my American Dream, my father will be un-chased by the dogs of society who seem determined to kill or simply draw blood for the sport of it. In the Antonito version of the American Dream Alfonzo Abeyta will be free of banks that lend more money to lesser men because they have "better" last names. Yes, George, I imagine the American Dream is only partially real and the good parts we wish for have been predestined to remain dreamlike, therefore fleeting and only attainable in the few minutes after we wake, but this should not keep us from our daily rising, the early dawn of each day when the earth chips away at the night and each of us opens our eyes to the pursuit of at least one of our dreams. The one dream, American or otherwise, that we must never run from.

Much peace Amigo,

a.

A Letter for the Unidentified Mexican National Who Died at 5:00 p.m. Somewhere Between San Luis and Manassa, His Van Rolling 3¼ Times

tonight i will name you Jose Molina
you are a butterfly in a pine tree
the curve of the mountain
the clouds that ring us
the stars above rubbing into them
a beautiful friction

tonight Jose Molina you are all that we deny
the green fields of the gringos as antonito burns
the dry conejos
the broken winged birds who migrate
to their same fence day after day
the ground beneath them
diamond filled with broken glass
el viejo Moeller saying
"while they drink wine i drink their water"

Jose Molina who came to this country
one of fifty five lying flat
shoulder to shoulder beneath the false floor of a semi
eighteen hours from vera cruz
where he was baptized in a pink church
is unidentified in today's paper
so that we might call ourselves spanish
and call him wetback
to make it easier to forget him
it is easier really
to be without hope and spanish
than forgotten and mexican

Jose Molina i have seen you before
your silhouetted body facing east
in the door frame of your trailer on a winter morning
trying to become warm
become american
able to tell yourself that you are not cold
tell yourself that a bird caught in fence
is living and not barely alive
that the well dug ten feet too shallow
is potential rather than a failed dream

the only thing that grows during a drought is irony
six generations ago
my abuelo's abuelo saved the mormons
from a winter that would have killed them
fed them with twenty-two of his own cows
for this he was given a tent

i hesitate to write this as much as
Moeller hesitated to steal land
as much as manassa offered water
to their burning neighbors

i am not a racist
nor am i color blind

that field is green
this one is brown

Jose Molina is a man
not a mexican national

the conejos in her old riverbed is dry
the last of her blood diverted north toward manassa

i am not crying for what my ancestors failed to do
i am learning to shout for what my children will need

i am not spanish more than i am mexican
i have not forgotten Jose Molina or my mother

Jose Molina is not your real name
you died poor and mexican in a time of drought

tonight the stars are rubbing themselves
against a distant wall of clouds
there is friction in the air
an electricity that promises
something loud and memorable

Some Measure of Mercy—Justice

A Letter to the Headwaters Regarding a Boy's Memory

Dear John,

For some reason I cannot shake the memory of a man I only knew for less than a month. I met him the summer I turned twelve; he lived with us and he shared a room with me. My grandpa hired him to help with the ranch, moving cattle and supplying the sheep camp during the summer months. His name was Billy. We found out, only a week after he left, that he was also a murderer.

The sheriff came to our door, a July morning, there had been rain the night before, one of those feminine rains whose wispy fingers left the earth dark and wet; the sheriff asked if we had heard from or seen Billy. It was obvious from the five police cars in the driveway that Billy had done something serious. We learned the blurry and somewhat specific details of a supposed confrontation with a man from Tres Piedras, a single gunshot, a body stuffed in a culvert, a stolen two-tone Chevy pulling a two horse trailer, also stolen. Immediately I knew the gun he had used, a lever action .30.30, a Winchester I had fired many times in Billy's company.

He first appeared toward the end of May. We were working in a makeshift corral at the base of San Antonio Mountain. At the edges of the corral the lambs were writhing in pain, bleating half-heartedly into a constant wind. Our faces were caked in dried and finely filtered sheep shit, dirt and blood from the work of castrating and then docking the tails of our most recent crop of lambs. To the uninitiated it was a brutal scene set against tangles of chamizo and gnarled trees that surrounded the woven wire corral. It was the wrong month to do this work, but we had always done it in May, the wind from the west, angry with its purpose of melting snow and lifting the entire earth into some horrible remolino of memory and dust. There were nearly 500 tails and bits of ears at our feet; the lambs suffered at the edges of the corral, their testicles pinched with a green rubber the size of a Cheerio, some of their tails cut just at the tip of bone, ears docked, half of the left ear completely removed and two notches cut into the underside of the right ear. Each lamb received their own variation of the process. Male lambs, los borregos, had their tails cut with a sharp knife, their nuts bound with the green rubber tourniquet which would shrivel them to dangling husks in a month or so, only their left ear docked. The female lambs, las hembras, received the green rubber on their tail, just an inch or so from their culito, for breeding purposes; both of their ears received the knife. This is where we first met Billy; he rode out of the trees on a paint horse and came into camp. I cannot recall who looked the most frightening, us, the fallen and pain riddled lambs, Billy's horse or Billy, but I do remember feeling sorry for his horse whose ribs were obvious and countable, hooves unshod, legs cut and scratched in more places than any of us could count.

Billy's accent was obvious and undeniable, Texas. He told us how he had ridden the horse all the way from Texas; his voice was such that maybe he expected us to disbelieve his story. My grandpa was never one to mince words, and for that I still resent and love him, but we knew it was his place to speak first.

"Someone should make you walk from Texas without eating," as he gestured toward the reduced to nothing horse that in some former life must have been quite beautiful.

We hired him because we needed help moving the animals to the high country, at least that is the excuse we used, but in retrospect, from this rise of memory, I now believe that my grandpa loved something about that horse's spirit and he simply wanted to nurse the paint back to health in the meadows that comprise the bottomlands of our ranch

Billy was another story all together. I imagine that he had never been beautiful. His hair was the color of rain-wet straw and he was only a shadow above five feet tall, his eyes were a muddy blue I had never seen before or since, and half of his right arm was missing. For whatever reason, I knew better than to ask about his stump of an arm. I can speculate that he was not born that way because of the scars just below the still functioning elbow, but I would have liked to have known the specifics of Billy's arm, if he buried it, if there was anything left to be buried, if it was a combine in Kansas or a sawmill in Mississippi or just a drunken west Texas back road car accident that claimed his arm. My family in the intervening years has Christened Billy, quite unoriginally I might add, as the One Armed Bandit.

I cannot shake this one particular image, the way he shouldered his rifle, the way the barrel rested in the small crook of elbow at the terminus of his devastated arm. This, most likely, was the last thing the man from Tres Piedras saw before Billy murdered him and drove off in the dead man's truck.

Now as I am writing this, as with almost everything I write, I think of my hometown; as for my community I can tell you this, Antonito is a temporary place for most people and for a few of us it is home, permanent as blood or powerful memory. This place, temporary as it may be to some, is my home. It is the work of writers to save, with our dreams and imagination, what others relegate to the forgotten. I don't know that there is anything redeemable in Billy, but I know that he treated me well and thanked us every time we fed him. More importantly, I see him now, as well as his horse, as this metaphor of sorts for my community. There are some that view us as the horse, formerly beautiful and worth saving and there are others that see us as Billy, never beautiful and only remembered for those unforgivable things that we have done.

I do not know what became of Billy beyond the immediate days after he murdered the man from Tres Piedras. I know they caught him in Reno, still driving the stolen truck and trailer. His paint horse must have been in tow, but there is no mention of the horse in the article. For weeks after the murder, my father was a vigilant guard of his family, and I still remember how he rushed into my room one morning after something accidently thudded against the wall; he was there to protect me, and I still love him for that gesture.

Finally, after the trial and Billy was sent to prison, my family home returned to its normal day to day routine; we no longer locked the door and my father no longer slept with a rifle by the bed. A peace prevailed and we seemed to mostly forget about Billy, the One Armed Bandit.

I can't tell you exactly why he came to me every time I considered this letter. I tried to omit him, but he was always there. He came out of the trees on his beaten yet still beautiful horse, just as he had 28 years ago and demanded, somehow, that I include him in this letter. In my thoughts of him, I also see him fishing, the two of us pushing through the willows on the banks of the Conejos River. He casts with his good arm and then tucks the rod under his other arm and reels the shiny spinner to shore, his fat horse following us up river and occasionally nudging his owner in the simple gesture that always means love. These are the postures I remember him in. In my thoughts of Billy he turns to me at a place where the river forks in three directions; he looks back over his right shoulder and he smiles at me. It isn't a smile of happiness or some innocent joy. It is a smile of knowing. It is a smile that tells me, even this man, this particular memory, this seemingly worthless moment, all of this, is worth saving.

> Much Peace.
> Your amigo,
> a.

To Whom It May Concern (Cami II):

In the telling there were three kings that came to visit the baby Jesus, each from a different land and following the same bright and luminescent star; their choice was clear, their path brightly lit by their intentions and the light of the star before them. They carried gifts, the gifts memorialized in song and scripture, gifts of gold, frankincense and myrrh. They came to the manger, because they were called there to honor the newborn king. The frankincense was a gift for kings, and it was laid before the baby, presumably within the child's reach. The second gift was gold and it was the gift of great power; it too was placed at arm's length. Finally, there was myrrh, the fragrant and rare perfume taken from the sap of an intentionally wounded tree. It was from this wound that the small thorny tree would bleed and it was this figurative blood that the third king collected and made into the perfumed oil he would take to Bethlehem. The myrrh was for the anointing of the dead; it seemed an illogical choice for a gift, especially a gift given to an infant. The king placed this third gift next to the sweet smelling frankincense and glittering gold. In the telling, the baby Jesus reached out his hand toward the gifts the Magi had brought, and in that moment he chose the myrrh; he knew his fate, even then. Why would the newborn king choose the gift that signified his death? Could he not be wooed by the gold of power or the frankincense used to consecrate so many temples? The choice of the baby Jesus, is, at least on the surface, illogical.

And then there is my cousin Cami, the person on whose behalf I write this letter. Looking back at her life from this promontory of perspective and hindsight it would appear, at least on the surface, that she too, like so many of us, had many great and wonderful gifts laid out before her; she is gregarious, funny, personable, loving, and beautiful. Yet, despite all this, her hand, it seems, is inclined toward the choices of ruin and frayed logic. Those that love her and those whose job it is to determine her fate will look toward her transgressions and weigh them against the other obvious and more intelligent choices they would have made. They may find her selfish and childish. They will judge her to be obstinate and wasteful with their trust and hope for her. Based on what they believe to be their own right choices they will see the squandered opportunity that they imagine(d) was and should be Cami's life.

It's true, Cami has broken the hearts of those that love her; they have reached into their own lives and hearts for a place to find forgiveness, tolerance and patience for the pain she has caused them. They do not understand her choices. It seems impossible to view her life and the pain she has endured as a gift of any sort. I am not saying that my cousin is Jesus, but I am saying that there is Jesus in all of us, the beautiful and inexhaustible spark. I am saying that Cami has that inexhaustible spark; anyone that has spent any time with her cannot help but feel it. Her gifts are numerous, her failing singular.

I see my cousin now, as she prepares for yet another encounter with the legal system. She sent me an email where she apologized for disappointing me. Her remorse is palpable for many reasons, and I do not find it to be selfish and self-serving. She knows, full well, that she has been down this road before. She knows in her inexhaustible heart that she was given chances and that those chances were compounded with more chances, but that she failed, somehow, to fulfill the hope and faith so many had put in her. In a word, those that love her are disappointed.

In my imagination and personal script of that night, I imagine, too, that the Magi, Joseph and Mary were also disappointed in the gift the baby Jesus chose. It must have seemed an irrational choice, but we know from what transpired afterward that the gift the baby chose was not a gift for him but a gift for us.

Cami, in my opinion, has given us a gift that we are yet to realize. Does this mean that I am happy that she faltered after being given so many chances? Does this mean that the fabric of trust so many had woven on her behalf is unfrayed? Does this mean that her latest transgression should be viewed as a sacrifice punctuated by suffering and pain? It means none of these things. It simply means that there is a part of Cami that is like Jesus and there is some seed in her actions, some parable of wisdom that will and must fall on fertile soil. It is the hope of all humankind, I believe, that such a seed always fall back into the dark and loamy earth so that good can grow from the errant seed dropped from the hand of suffering.

All of us have experienced the pain of loss, betrayal, broken heartedness and disappointment; it seems as though our human condition demands that our joy be tempered, always, by some ache. I challenge anyone that reads this to look back upon the seed of their pain, the moment it fell from the sower's hand into the reaper's future and, in that moment, trace the arc of that particular falling to the person you are today, and I would argue that so many of us have found there is a bloom there, a fruit, ripe and sweet, from the kernel we thought was only and entirely made of despair. The world we live in is replete with equal parts sorrow and joy. For every temporary victory there is a longing that brings the kite of hope back to the earth from whence it came; we must find the gift in the fall, understand that sometimes the fall is a choice born of knowing, but born so we can know the redemption of the rising.

It is my opinion that the pain and heartache of Cami's past did not re-enter our lives that day; there was no relapse of the former self. I also believe that my cousin was not guilty, at least in my estimation, of anything other than a relapse of poor judgment. I am not condoning what she did, not giving her a pass for keeping poor company, nor am I suggesting that she is without fault. I am simply saying that she made a choice that even she does not understand.

I don't think it was a moment of weakness or betrayal that led me to this letter and the defense of my first cousin. The fact that Cami did not have drugs in her system speaks to her intent at the moment in question. I have known Cami too long to think she was naïve or unaware of the potential consequences of her actions; I simply believe that she acted without malevolence or intent to break the law, or perhaps more significantly, break the hearts of those that love her. Honestly, I believe she considered her actions of that moment to be benevolent, helping out a friend (a dubious "friend" who, in my estimation took advantage of her). That is the Cami I have always known, too nice, too gregarious, too beautiful and too loving. Her choices are always filtered by her nature, her human nature to be loved and to love. It is a tragic and beautiful irony; Cami's brightness is both her salvation and her sin.

I ask that you examine, closely, the entire person before you. Please take into account the better person and citizen Cami has become in the past two years. It is true, the renewed fabric that is her life has places where the thread shows through, the hand of the sewer unsteady and unsure at times, the starts and the stops most visible in the places where the filament has met the hem in a crooked line. The colors of her restoration are not the ones we would have chosen; they sit bright, juxtaposed and glaring to what we would have done, but the garment, I assure you, is complete and sewn with benign intent; there is no malice in the pattern. Did she, knowingly betray all those that love her, those that had placed so much new hope in her, those that helped place the thread of repair and restoration in her hand? I do not think so. I think she simply made a mistake. I contend that Cami's choice of that moment, the ill-fated moment we cannot reconcile as a wise choice, is the moment we were pushed toward a higher understanding and patience we, her family, are not yet capable of. I know it does not seem that way now, nor has it seemed as such in the recent past, but there is a gift in this despair, some bloom whose fragrance we are yet to recognize.

The myrrh is harvested from a wounded tree. The sap that flows toward the wound, to heal the injury, is known as tears. The myrrh is born of injury. The myrrh is what one of the Magi brought the child king. The myrrh is a gift, sweet and fragrant.

Sincerely,
Aaron A. Abeyta

A letter to the parents of the San Luis Valley

Dear Parents,

South of Antonito, as you drop down from the mesa into the village of Ortiz, just north of the Los Pinos River, there is a mound of dirt. The mound of dirt is overgrown in every season with tall grass that catches the wind. To the west there is an abandoned house and a corral made of split logs. To the south, across the river, there is an abandoned house with only two adobe walls standing. To the east there are two houses where people still live, and further east there are meadows that extend along the river until they reach the rocky mesa that surrounds Ortiz. If you are not paying attention you will not even see this mound of dirt. By the time I am an old man it will exist only in memory.

Each of you is here today because you want success for your children. You want their education to serve them well. You want for your children to grow into a world where they will make a significant contribution. In this vein I've been asked to talk today about parental involvement in student learning.

We've all heard it hundreds of times; ultimately a conversation will turn towards the state of education. Too often the language of this conversation points at failures large and small, but mostly the conversation falls into a tug of war where the rope between differing views is blame. Parents blame administrations and teachers and the schools blame parents for not caring enough. Even listening to the sound of that last statement seems odd to me. Arguably there are parents who do not care for their children, but everyone in this room knows better than that. An overwhelming majority of parents care deeply about their child's learning and education.

West of Antonito there is a place where the road narrows between the Conejos river and the flanks of Mogote Peaks. On either side there is not much room to maneuver beyond where the road takes you. My father is driving east. I know from experience the story he will tell when the truck passes through this narrow place where geography, human work, and memory meet. There will be a story about sheep flowing off the mountain toward the river where they will drink before ascending the mountain once again, only to return two days later to drink again. Above us and out of sight the mountain slopes toward the skyline and the openness of the mountain's northern side. This is where my father, then a boy, and other boys like him, herded sheep with a man named Carrillo. In the world outside of my father's memory, Carrillo is not important.

For me school was close to torturous. I do not think that people keep official record of such suffering, but if there were a written record somewhere it would note that I might well hold several world records for visiting the principal's office. It wasn't that I was a bad kid, and it wasn't that I was a product of a bad home or a poor town. My world records would include schools in Pueblo, Taos, Cheyenne and, yes, Antonito. As a twenty-five year old man I even managed to get sent to the office once for wearing a cap in school. I had been invited to do a poetry reading at East High School in Cheyenne, Wyoming and decided I should get there early. As I walked in the teacher on duty complimented me on the appearance of my hat. He said something very profound like "Nice hat." The sarcasm of his voice and the school's dress code were both lost on me. I simply replied "thanks" and continued to walk toward the classroom where I was scheduled to read. Needless to say, I was grabbed by my right arm and was being tugged toward a principal's office that I thought I had left in my tortured days as a student.

Perhaps torture is a strong word. No one forced pieces of bamboo under my fingernails and I only had one teacher who still thought it was okay to paddle kids. I was lucky because he was old and I was still young enough to outrun him. In the eyes of the schools I attended I was a bad kid. Truthfully, I was not a bad kid; I wasn't bored, and most of all my parents never missed parent teacher conferences or any of my extracurricular activities. The real truth was that school did not matter to me.

The mound of dirt is the size of a small room. It is approximately three feet higher than the earth it rises from. If we are talking truths then the opposite would be lies. It would be a lie and it would also be the truth if I told you that a nondescript mound of dirt, overgrown with grass, is the reason why I think education matters. It would be both truth and lie if I told you that this mound of dirt equals something like your participation in the academic life of your son or daughter. The truth of this metaphor is that parental involvement is easily overlooked. The lie is that your involvement is as small and inconsequential as a tiny rise in the earth, almost non-existent.

As a boy I didn't know the mound of dirt existed. As a boy I didn't know it mattered. As a man it is the reason someone saw fit to invite me here today.

Perhaps you are wondering where all of this will lead. Perhaps you are concerned that I have lost it altogether and will go on for 30 minutes about the dimensions of a mound of dirt. Maybe some of you are wondering how on earth I could be an English teacher because my essay is as scattered as valley dust in a windy spring. If any of these statements mirror your concerns I will get to the point as best I can. I'm not here to tell you how to help your child with their calculus or English homework. I'm here for one reason, to tell you how it was that education began to matter in my life. The day that education finally mattered to me was the day I discovered that my history, our collective history, the well of deep water that is your family history, the cultural, religious, and community histories of this valley are what made me real.

I went off to college where I was known by my social security number and a special nine digit number that was called my student number. I left a high school where I was a full time student and represented enrollment numbers which, in turn, translated to funding for the school. I left a locker full of books that did not mention me or my ancestors and walked into the biggest bookstore I had ever seen and bought four hundred dollars worth of books that still claimed I did not exist. My parents had pushed me to get good grades. They were active in my life and talked regularly with my teachers, but nothing I studied made me whole. Now, years later, I go back to the schools I once attended and see that curricula hasn't changed. Now, years later, I teach college and we are given certain guidelines by the state on what we should teach in certain classes. Again, there is no mention of me, you, your family, your culture, your religion, your history. You can ask a hundred educators and most, if not all of them, will tell you that the current educational system is not geared toward poor, rural, or inner city communities. I don't mean to deliberately sound pessimistic, but there is little, in terms of obvious value, for our students to relate to in today's educational climate. This is not to say that there is no meaningful learning taking place, though some may argue that CSAP and other high stakes tests have limited teachers in terms of creativity and teaching beyond the rote memorization skills being drilled in too many classrooms. If anything CSAP and tests like it have finally given parents and teachers a common "enemy."

The herd of sheep rolled off the mountain like morning fog and clogged the road. As some sheep reached the edge of the river others had already had their fill and were returning toward the mountain. Carrillo had a dog that was legend among all the herders. His dog was trained to follow its master's hand gestures. I never knew Carrillo or his dog, but I see him here today as though I was there to watch him remove his hat and switch it from left hand to right, each gesture some broad stroke of an artist whose craft is almost absent from this area. The dog would turn and follow the motion of Carrillo's hands as if there were invisible strings connecting the two. As Carrillo sat atop his horse he guided the dog along the side of the road, clearing it for the vehicles that had come upon the commotion. There was one vehicle, in particular, that seemed to be in some great hurry, a truck, with Texas plates, pulling a camper. As the dog cleared the road the truck followed noisily behind, honking, engine revved, and when there seemed to be a small break in the swarm of sheep the truck rushed through. The driver of the truck did not stop after it had run over Carrillo's dog.

The dog lay there motionless, completely dead. As the truck sped away Carrillo yelled after it. Perhaps he acted irrationally; he loved his dog, the rifle removed from the scabbard, a quick aim, three shots. Carrillo spent a few years in prison. He went to work for a rancher when he got out. He was not the same man. My father tells his story still. How the man from Texas ran over the greatest dog anyone had ever seen. How the man in the truck was only injured by the erratic shots, and how Carrillo returned from prison and was killed by a horse that kicked him in the head.

That mound of dirt. It is the house where my mother was born. It is the withered adobes fallen to rubble and then ground to dust. It is the last of the home where my mother was born. The abandoned house to the west is where my wife's family was raised. The fallen house to the south with only two walls standing was the home of my great uncle Willie. Every turn in every road, every adobe, standing or fallen, has a story that makes education important. Like my mother's birth house, the language and customs of my people is slowly crumbling to an unrecognizable and overgrown mound of crumbled adobes. There are things that every culture is losing. Every culture will or has already been forced to check a multiple choice box that makes them either right or wrong. Standardized tests do not care about the hill where young boys herded sheep. These tests do not concern themselves with natural features of any home and the stories each feature holds. Here is where the parents must become actively involved. Here is where the parents must make education, not only multi-dimensional but multi-generational as well. For example, I am not good at math, but my ancestors, centuries ago, had calendars, star charts, and mathematical knowledge that exceeded anything seen in Europe. I do not like math, but it means something to me because it has been made part of me by education, by family, by heritage, by the responsibility handed down for generations. This is the very same gift you can give your child. The very same gift that will make their education relevant. You don't have to make them love it, only understand how it is part of their lives already.

Parental involvement, that is why we are here. Maybe it is narrow-minded of me to think that today's society is completely concerned with its version of individuality. We are a society predicated on making everything newer and faster. CSAP and other high stakes testing now pre-determines for us what schools are doing their job and by association what parents care about their children the most. My suggestions for parental involvement will never be cited as a way to boost test scores, but I'm willing to bet that if a student were to take ownership of their history, culture, and the inherent responsibilities of each, that scores would go up.

Parents, all the parents of this valley, and I mean that with the full force of both its meanings. As parents you are the keepers of history, not only of your family but of this valley. Your involvement with your children is the history you share with them. In the end, this essay is not about a mound of dirt or a sheepherder who was sent to prison, but to this day, every time I open a book, read a poem, or lecture on some seemingly abstract concept I know that somewhere, buried deep in the recesses of the canon of European literature, is a character who loves completely what is lost. Or there is some character whose only quest is to find their home and be reunited with their loved ones. Every time I read of some great Greek god and their amazing powers I will somehow, I can't trace the origins, think of the way my abuelita survived a Great Depression, 13 children and a husband that died too young.

Education is about finding your home. That is essentially what a major is. That is what a course of study is. Education is about finding your place in this world. I argue that this place is already within each of us. As a young student I did not know this. My parents told stories. My grandparents told stories. The trees carved with names told stories and I did not listen like I should have. I was lucky because the people that loved me did not cease in their storytelling.

Later, when I went off to become more educated I knew my connection to my learning was strong because my parents had taught me where it was that I belonged. Someday I may live across an ocean, as may some of your children. Their lives may be tossed on the open water of some turbulent wave. You should not fear for them; their boat will be strong and seaworthy. For me the boat is a mound of dirt and a narrow place where sheep came to drink river water. For your child there will be something else, something that no schoolbook holds, something that a teacher will never put on the board, some equation whose solution is not decipherable with a calculator. You will hear it many times, a call for parents to be more active in the education of their children. By all means if you can help with calculus, then please do so. If you can help with a book report then please do so, but more than that you may want to teach your child where they belong in the world, how their life is important and part of a cycle and history that cannot be delivered in a lecture or chapter summary. Ultimately, the role of the parent, as I see it, is to be a parent to a child and a place, to nurture both so that the two will always know they are related, so they will know that education and family are a shared responsibility in much the same way that place and its people are a shared responsibility. We are linked to our place because we are this place. There is no difference between this link and the education you will give your child. Like a home that lives within us, it cannot be taken away, lost, or stolen.

Sincerely,

aaron

A Letter to the Headwaters from the Radical Center

Dear John,

Quite often I am left at a loss when asked to write about the various Headwaters topics, their subjects often feeling as foreign as a splinter under the flesh. Today is different though, the cool of autumn is settling into the valley, the windows have frost in the mornings, the crops have been put away to their winter homes, and the sheep have come down from the high country. I often think it miraculous or at least intriguing how one day the sheep just seem to materialize, how their bodies flow into a meadow like a jubilant fog of bleating and baahing.

So anyway, the radical center . . . unexpected partnerships, perhaps one such partnership is our Cuban sheepherder, a Castro reject of the Muriel Boat Lift, "flushed" upon our country some three decades ago. I have never fully understood the progression of circumstances and that brought him to Colorado, to Antonito, to the arms of his Mexican partner, she herself an immigrant of a different sort, brought here as one of 55 under the false bottom of a semi. I often wonder what invisible hand guided them here to each other and to my family. I believe that the moment they left their homes and family, quite literally forever, they left their place for this radical center known as the United States. Just so we are clear, this isn't a patriotic love song about melting pots, complete with a chorus of loss and assimilation sung to the tune of some greater good and ultimate gain. I guess what I am saying here is that I understand the radical center, these partnerships of necessity and cooperation. You see John, the radical center, the misunderstood nebula of the center is where the poor, the lost, the weak, the disenfranchised, and the marginalized have always lived. They have been forced to exist and sometimes thrive there, at the bulls eye of the board where the bitter and random darts of hatred, racism, misunderstanding and cultural incompetence, to name just a few, are set upon their trajectory in order to find their mark at the radical center of the board where my people and the people like them have inhabited for generations. Put another way, it is the American minority that has created the radical center. Our daily life is a practice in radical compromise, forced always to straddle the two circumstances of identity we've come to accept as our lives; we must constantly choose which side to inhabit. Our safety, well-being, and daily breath mandate that we live in the radical center. W.E.B. DuBois called it twoness and I believe he knew exactly what this center looked like. He identified it as *two souls, two thoughts, two unreconciled strivings; two warring ideals in one dark body, whose dogged strength alone keeps it from being torn asunder.*

The unexpected partnerships that the participants of Headwaters are applying to the environment are remarkably similar to the partnership, not always symbiotic and sometimes destructive, that the American immigrant and minority must contend with on a daily basis. We/they are forced to walk the fragile bridge between two cultures and ideologies. If we are concerned with a "resilient future" and with the "break from traditional stereotypical positions" in order to transcend diverging political views, we need to look to the most stereotyped and resilient people our country has to offer, the poor and the marginalized. The map we seek to some transcendent enlightenment is not often found in books or libraries; instead, the map is a permanent record of survival and strength written into the souls and memories of the very people that so many Americans wish to drive out.

A small part of me is angry that an Arizona rancher is given credit for this radical center, that our place of survival is now being colonized and blurred. It is changed only by context but not by effect or intent. The radical center became the amorphous kingdom of the immigrants the moment they chose to leave everything and everyone they have ever known in order to become American. The center became theirs every time a teacher beats their native language from their tongues with the colonial whips of assimilation. The center became theirs every time the politicos pander for their votes but leave their schools and communities to crumble. The center, by necessity and desire, is the river the flames cannot leap over.

Well John, I have gone on forever now. My guess is that you have grown weary of my rambling and accusations. I will leave you on a more positive note. Michele and I are parents now. Our house is filling with toys and sound; there is a third laughter now. Her name is Rut, but we call her Ruth because most Americans cannot stop calling her rut. She is a beautiful Ethiopian girl, five years old and so much like Michele it is all at once eerie and transcendent that two souls could match up so, separated by over 8000 miles, two continents and an ocean. It's true, there was much heartache before Rut arrived and we tell her of her siblings in heaven. She is our earthly child now, sent to us by some seemingly random plan stitched together by phone calls and fate. She knows she is from Africa, from a place called Mykelle. She uses both of our last names. She knows that we have given her my grandmother's name as her middle name. Already children have refused to play with her because of her skin color. You see John, all of these unexpected partnerships are sometimes won with hard work and sweat. Other times they are won with tears and the fraying fabric of grief. Sometimes they come in prayer and wish. Mostly though, they come as a combination of all these things; each is a necessary component of the partnership. Somewhere between the grief and the sweat laced with prayer there is a common ground that makes us human.

It is early. Soon my family will wake and it will be too loud for writing. Rut will rub the sleep from her large and beautiful eyes. She will hug her mother and me. She will be unaware, for the time being, of the radical center she inhabits between two worlds. I am happy. Autumn is vibrant and very much alive. The sheep are fat in the field. I am smiling. I have just figured out that center is a place where love can sing to us from what we presumed to be a dark place.

Much Peace,

a.

a letter to Pablo about hope

And one morning it was all ablaze,
and one morning firestorms
erupted from the earth
and from then on, flames,
and in the streets the blood of children
flowed simply, like blood from children.
　　　　　　　　—*Pablo Neruda*

this earth
whose rain and locomotive whistles you loved
is burning once again
and in the streets
they mostly show women with pictures
who look upward
and that is why i call this letter hope

have you already heard
was it the birds
who under their wings
bring autumn from the north
one cold morning at a time
or was it the smoke
filled with gray screams
of a history that repeats itself

right now i am wondering
which sign i should follow
i could not find paper
but there was that other voice
which pointed to this piece of cardboard
Pablo there must be poets everywhere

trying to explain a few things
and now we know why simile fails
when she is dressed in flames

here it has rained during the night
and in new york
it is also raining and a friend says
even the birds have stopped.
here the sky is calm
and the birds line themselves
on the fences notes of music
and in the early fog
of the cooling earth they begin again
and still i cannot explain the streets
nor do i know why
the birds would quit their singing

Pablo   tell me
is there an image
that word capable a gesture for flames
and another for people who hope
despite the smoke
because *in the streets*
people wait like people waiting
and perhaps they wish their pictures
were not of suits dresses and smiles
but of some deep earth of ash
so we might really know
from the paper taped to the bus stop vestibule
who is sleeping and who is sleeping
beyond the last days of summer
with her shrinking days

here is a truth i am afraid
the wound will remind itself of its origins

did the earth
has the earth
will it ever forgive itself
for its fire
Pablo
i am here with my pen
i wish it were green
it is the color of the sky before a storm
so i write to you knowing
that a poem with its
heartbeats of syllables
can change nothing
yet *words keep on*
simply like words that must keep on
in them too there is hope
that looks up towards things
and the word on two feet
tries to build again
even when no one listens

dear Pablo
your birthplace of oceans
is trying to forgive itself
as the men work in the rain
and 2000 miles away i am writing
on the back of a piece of cardboard
hoping
that anything dressed in anger
will not repeat itself

i know it will
and that is why *in the streets*
the poets must at least try
we must at the very least
remind the sky
that there is something like prayer
in the smoke
and that soon enough
the birds will begin again

Ella—The Land

A Letter to the Headwaters Concerning What is Not There

To the east of Antonito there are great meadows, and in the summer the grass comes up to a man's waist. Beyond the meadows the llano unfolds with its sprawl of sage, dust devils, brief shadows and the ever present wind. The line between the meadows and the llano is abrupt, as though God simply grew tired or ran out of paint. The line between the two is the place where the great shore of brown runs up against a sea of green.

The real difference between the two, however, is water. The meadows with their thick clover and dancing brome cling to the rivers and acequias. Culverts and head gates, with their straight lines and steel, attempt to bring order to the dark ribbons of melt water running in the fields, the impossibly twisted cottonwoods along the river, the snarled and thorny champe bushes turning thick red and sweet along the ditches. The meadows are a great spill of life. The llanos are this vast desert of volcanic rock, ghostly antelope gliding in and out of mirages, beetles and rattlesnakes sunning themselves in the floury dust that clings to everything. The two landscapes and the stark line between them is the place where prosperity attempts to redefine itself.

Before I was born the meadows and fields extended nearly ten miles further to the east. When I was a boy my father would point out the skeletons of abandoned farm equipment, the bleached and whitened bones of ditches carved into the side of the mesas. The llano and white sage have retaken what is rightfully theirs, but in the early blood of dawn or when the light is just right, you can see the perpendicular and horizontal lines, the scars of what used to be miles upon miles of peas, oats, and barley. These lines are the demarcations of some lost and forgotten hope made real by the abandoned and hollow wishes of abandoned homes. Most of the homes are made of stone and good lumber. They have two levels, sometimes three. It is obvious that the owners intended to stay forever.

That word, forever, is a paradox. For that matter, so too is prosperity. Were those words ever meant to be uttered in Antonito where things seem to disappear in the flash and swirl of a pen, the draining of a bottle, in the echo of a departing train whistle? Forever is temporary here. Prosperity, redefined or otherwise, is just another way of saying temporary. These homes, these ditches, this llano, all of it are proof of that.

Cove Lake is still on the maps; it is long and blue. It has been gone for nearly 50 years now. The locals joke about the occasional kayaker or fisherman that comes in looking for directions to the lake. They seem amazed when they are told that the lake no longer exists. They point at it on their maps as though that might jar our memory and make the lake reappear. It might be humorous if it weren't so sad, an entire lake, a viable economy, a way of life, sold away in a water compact with Texas.

I guess my issue with this idea of redefining prosperity is that I don't really understand it. There, I've admitted it. How can a place or people redefine what they've never really known? How can a new and viable economy emerge from the ashes of every other failed dream? I don't mean to be fatalistic. I want to be hopeful, but prosperous is something the people of Antonito are not allowed to be. We work hard, our imagination and ingenuity are strong, but every great idea we have is stolen or stonewalled. The cost of poverty is not the lack of things, the true cost of poverty is that you are not even allowed to possess ideas or given the means to make them come about. Cove Lake and those abandoned fields are just one example. There was a time when tens of thousands of sheep were raised in and around Antonito. Those too are gone, loaded on a train nearly 80 years ago, the profits and prosperity of countless families shipped north to the sale barns of northern Colorado, the money pocketed and stolen by the agent who pretended to be our friend.

Maybe, in all of this, these lines of meadow and llano, these scars of forgotten fields, the twisted spines of abandoned ditches and crumbling frames of semi-permanent dreams lies the point. Maybe prosperity should not be determined by acre feet of water, bank rolls and possessions. Maybe the true prosperity of a place is its people and its memory. Sometimes they are all we have left. I wish, in the un-definable X of my soul, that prosperity were not about money or power. But I will be honest, I don't know what prosperity is. I've never really known it. I don't think Antonito has either. I didn't grow up poor. We had what we needed, but I can't remember a time when my mother's and father's paychecks did not go directly into the ranch they struggle, to this day, to keep afloat.

I guess I need help. All the ideas of prosperity I've known are crumbled now. I don't equate monetary things with success or wealth, but I don't see the paradigm shift either. Prosperity means money and redefining it means earning money in a different way, one that is more eco friendly or not driven by corporate America. Either way a person or place needs capital, a foundation from which they can redefine their prosperity, but that leads to the real question. How can you redefine what is not there to begin with? How do you make the bones human again? I really want to know. I'm here at the edge of the meadow, my boots are caked in dust and there is a stiff wind in my face. Behind me there are a million ghosts, they stoop to fill their bushel baskets with peas, they call out to one another from the abandoned rows of forgotten fields. They want to know too. Their voices disappear like smoke in a hard wind. You can barely hear them. They are asking all of you what they have done wrong, they are asking where they have gone wrong. They are asking you for some glimmer of hope, some new thing with which to fill their baskets.

Much Peace,

a.

A Letter to Leopold Upon Reading "The River of the Mother of God"[1]

Dear Aldo,

The mountains to the east are the color of folds in a blue garment or the darkness of a river in winter, where blue presses up against the hilt of black, and I have come to the house that you built, over 100 years ago, because I have heard that you were a prophet, not of the coming of Christ like Jeremiah and Isaiah, but a sybil of the hearts of men, a diviner of the desire folded into every human heart, whose secret is often revealed in the fire that men call progress. I am here to finish a book of letters and it seems fitting that this one be written to you, a man who was visionary enough to build upon a slight hill and place the largest window where it could look east.

To my right there is a church, roof of tin and walls painted an orangish yellow of sherbet or a weak sunset. It is not like most churches, the door does not face east. As a child my wife attended a wedding in that church, we wonder, together, if the marriage has persisted, blessed as it was in such a small church; was God more present there? I believe he was. You would have to love this place to choose such a church for marriage. There are larger churches in Taos, a cathedral in Santa Fe, but someone loved completely where they were from and chose that church, sent out invitations to the meager few that would fit inside and my wife so many years later remembers coming there with her grandparents; there is nothing but love in her recollection. I believe in the part of my heart I have saved for good, that the marriage lasted and the couple is watching this very sunset. The sky has a way of connecting all of us, the light that reminds us of when we were younger.

Childhood is over thirty years ago now, depending on how a person measures the extinction of such things as innocence. I am writing

1 This letter was written in late December 2013, during Aaron's residency at the "Mi Casita" Residency built by Aldo and Estella Leopold in the early twentieth century. Special thanks go to the US Forest Service, the Aldo Leopold Foundation, and the Rocky Mountain Land Library.

at December dusk, one week removed from the shortest day of the year; the sky, at the horizon, is orange, white and silver. I, too, am thinking of my youth and the wilderness you had a hand in shaping after God, wind, water, time and the light had done their work.

I was seven when the roads to Cruces Basin were closed for good. Before that we would descend an eastern road toward the lowest end of the basin, where all the water would meet before tumbling north and east into Toltec gorge. The road was carved into the slope of a mountain, serpentine, steepest at the beginning and at the end, a road crowded with aspen and the names of men carved into the trees. The names still exist having grown and scarred black, raised and rough to the touch, into the bone skin of aspen. The road is a faint trail now, appearing to the uninitiated as a game trail, but you and I know that no animal would take such a circuitous route to any place. Only humans have the distinction of folding a road upon itself, appearing as if it is an abandoned ribbon dropped from some immortal hand and left to become this spiral of dirt dropping toward the place where water merges. I do not think you a prophet, per se, but I believe you are accurate in your characterization of roads. What was it you said of such things, "Frankenstein" and "And of all foolish roads, the most pleasing is the one that 'opens up' some last little vestige of virgin wilderness."

The adults would sit in the cab of the Ford pickup, and the rest of us would pile into the back among the stock salt, shovels, and propane tanks. The load varied in weight only; our cargo as predictable as snowmelt in May and snowfall in October. We carried cans of creamed corn, a whole chicken, steaks cut thick, a box of bacon ends, 200 pounds of sheep salt, 80 pounds of oats for Rex and Baby Doll, a steel trough made from a dissected water heater and welded with legs of half inch pipe; we carried ginger snaps, cartons of eggs wrapped and in old blankets to preserve them against the jarring ride our youthful bodies did not notice; there was a bag of pinto beans, one pound of lard, two pounds of table salt, a forty pound bag of dog food for Pancho and Smokey, cans of peaches in heavy syrup, a bag of lentils, a carton of Lucky Strikes, cans of potted meat and Vienna sausages, one box of powdered donuts, a gallon of kerosene, one magazine we were not allowed to look at but did anyway; there were .22 shells and .30.30 cartridges. We carried only what we thought a grown man, two horses, two dogs and 1000 sheep would need for a week, and we would descend the road to where Diablo Creek meets Beaver Creek. We would cry out, loud, against the canyon walls, listen as if amazed as our "hey" would return to us, this boomerang of sound that filled us as it diminished. We would cry out for the echo's sake but also so the herder would know we were close. We had learned it was not always in the interest of young boys, even in the company of grown men, to arrive unannounced.

His name was Roger Arellano, and he was our herder for most of my young life; he was thin as reeds of grass, his chaps were so thick it appeared as if they might be heavy enough to buckle him in two, but he sat a horse better than any man I have ever known. All of our horses seemed to love him.

When we came upon the camp of our herder we found it empty, only the remnants of a morning fire warmed the box stove; there were wisps of silver smoke that lingered in the spruce. The day was clear. Everything had to it a smell of ancient things. We found him bathing in a deep bend of Diablo Creek, just down a slight slope from where his horse was grazing; we found him naked save for his white Stetson, his ivory buttoned shirt, boots and spurs, white cotton socks, Levi's and chaps were in a neat pile. There were two backpacks, two shirts, neither with sleeves, one orange and the other turquoise, two pair of hiking shorts and two pair of hiking boots, all strewn casually in the grass of Cruces Basin. The naked women were standing when we arrived, the soft water of the creek spiraled and clung near their knees and then let go and flowed downstream. Both women wore braids in their yellow hair, tied with white and blue strips of cloth, both women were slightly larger than Roger, who was seated and smiling, his back against a western bank of the creek, as he watched them bathe. Roger stood and greeted us, and the women turned and did the same. Only the watchers seemed to feel embarrassment. I remember that story now. I was the youngest, too young to witness such things, but later, as the canyon filled with bird noise and sheep calling to their lambs, Roger came up to me and asked if I knew why it was New Mexico was called the land of enchantment. I insisted with my eyes that I did not. He pointed off to the south, and at the edge of the meadow you could make out the two women as they hiked toward Rincon Bonito. Their orange and turquoise shirts barely visible behind their large packs, their bodies juxtaposed against the spruce and tall grass. He smiled. I smiled, not entirely sure why. He patted me on the back and 38 years later, though I never saw the two women again, there is a bend in Diablo Creek in the Cruces Basin Wilderness where the motto of New Mexico came to be.

Long after the road to Cruces Basin had been closed, as Roger grew older, there was a Palomina named Daisy; she loved him with a loyalty that was unconditional, following him everywhere, answering his whistle call, grazing untethered and returning every morning. She was a beautiful horse, so gold that in certain light she appeared to be made of snow. During the summer we would swap out horses every month, the toil of a working animal would measure itself on each of them; they would grow thin from the constant work and the limited feed, only able to consume what they could reach at the end of their picket and rope. Daisy was different though; she refused to leave him, was never tethered and she did not grow thin.

A few years passed, it was the spring of my freshman year in high school, and Roger did not come back to work; he told us that he was retiring. I saw him once more. He had come to my abuelita's funeral, and as we were leaving the church I remember that, this hero of a previous youth asked my grandpa for five dollars.

That first summer after he retired, the man who replaced Roger shot and killed Daisy. She did not die right off, but the bullet was lodged deep in her hind quarter and it was my job, the youngest of the boys, to walk her out of the wilderness and up to the road on Brazos Overlook so we could load her in the truck; when she was healthy that walk should have taken less than an hour, but she limped as though every part of her was about to come undone. The veterinarian said the bullet was too deep, her blood already infected by the lead; she died two weeks later in the bosque south of my abuelito's house. The new herder claimed that he mistook Daisy for a bear, as she walked through the flock one night; we knew the story of the bear was a lie. We speculated that he grew angry, the palomina refusing to answer his call or be caught by this man who could not ride. That is the way with certain men. Hearts fill quickly, regardless of who we are or where we come from, a poisoned heart can kill something without a second thought. It is the poison that seems to justify the end.

None of us were stupid enough to believe that a bear could grow to be so gold, so tall, with a tail that, in the right light, appeared to be made of razor fine sunlight breaking through shadow. We knew, too, that a horse can love a human, and even a boy can know that a broken heart, those of the animal sort, are often irreparable.

It is there in the narrow meadows of Cruces Basin where I always remember that horse, gold as morning light, prospering. She was beautiful, and sometimes I miss her.

Roger died of what ails old men in his line of work, loneliness chief among them. Also, there was too much alcohol and being too generous with his paychecks. And then there was his back, broken in four places by an auger that caught his clothing and sucked him into a combine when he was a young man. He showed us the scars now and again, spiral rivers of flesh lighter than the dark skin of his torso, the banks of his river of disfigurement seemed smooth as places where meadow meets water, but as the scars spun toward his back there was evidence of what true violence is, deep divots of missing flesh, craters of pocked and clawed away flesh. All of these things must have contributed to his death, but put another way, Roger died of what was missing in his life. I sometimes pray for him and for his Daisy. I hope they are together. I hope heaven is like a wilderness where all the horses are un-tethered and come running to the sound of a sharp whistle against canyon.

Roger Arellano walked as though he was afraid to leave footprints; he appeared to be made of leaves, pollen and fine dust, but he was human. He is dead now, nearly 20 years. I loved him then and do now.

Mr. Leopold, it seems that at this moment, all the memories of my childhood, the truest and best of them, in some way or another lead me to the Cruces Basin Wilderness you championed, envisioned and undoubtedly rode during your time in Tres Piedras. This home of yours has pictures of you scattered throughout, almost all of them show you in the outdoors. You are either stoic or smiling. The pictures do what pictures should; I feel I know you because of their silence and your gaze in them. In some of the photos there is a horse, in one of them there is a dog. It would seem that you preferred your boots on the outside of your pants, that your boots be square toed, your dogs to be shepherds and able to handle the cold, and that your horses be small and nimble.

Truth be told, I do not think of you as a prophet; rather, I believe you knew that thing Aristotle used to describe character, "man is his desire." You knew that in our quest to make known every fold of mountain, every blue line of map, every uncharted shadow of place, that we would smooth over our imaginations with what we profess to have learned from the prying of our hands into the chest of wild places, our pulling apart the sternum of the unknown and looking upon the four chambered engine of what we fear most, silence, failure, peace and anonymity.

I suppose that somewhere there exists a silent road, and we have done our best to make that road and others like it stand for imagination and longing, done our part to construct what is loudest and fastest into the standard for longing and the promise of some predetermined arrival already worked out by average speeds, average delays, miles per gallon, distance, traffic and a knowledge of what we will experience once we get there. Even

Everest, as you predicted, is mapped, climbed from more aspects than previously imagined. Mallory has been found on the northeast flank of the mountain, his mummified body lying face down in the scree, one leg obviously broken from his fall of nearly a century ago; his other leg folded over the broken part of his body. Perhaps the final comfort he would ever know was the consolation that gesture brought him. What most threatens our silence and therefore our imagination is the very thing that first inspired both. You compared our desire to the potato bug that exterminated the potato and therefore exterminated itself, and while that is not the romantic analogy that any of us would expect or assign to our own hunger, I feel that you are not far from the truth with that observation. If desire is hunger and hunger is the work of human hearts, then I fear there is nothing that can satiate such an animal. What a cruel and beautiful thing to know, that our demise is incalculably worked into the equation of our longing.

I thank you for building this house, for this window, for laying the groundwork for certain roads to be closed to anything with a motor. I thank you for that descent into the Cruces Basin, for the fallen logs, the switchbacks that have grown over to grass, and I thank you for the young and unmarked, pristine, trees. There is no way you could have known Roger Arellano, but I thank you for parts of my memory of him, too. You left this place even before he was born. I read somewhere that you were struck down by nephritis while attempting to soothe over a dispute between cattlemen and sheepmen. In truth, you were most likely settling a dispute over new fences and land sold and lost without notice. You were settling a row of human hearts and possession of said heart; the very same battle still persists today. I imagine the dispute happened west of this home, in the mountains of the Carson National Forest, perhaps somewhere near Cruces Basin. I visualize that you rode a small horse and that a good dog followed behind. I read that you almost died because of the infection in your kidneys. At the moment when you knew you were sick and needed to return home, I imagine that all you really needed to do was turn your horse toward home and it was her own longing that carried you both back to this place. That is what I love most about horses, they can forgive almost anything if they trust you will let them return home and they sense that you are not of a cruel heart. I ramble here, but I wonder sometimes what would happen if the earth and just a few humans were as forgiving as horses.

The sun is down. The sky is pink with alpenglow. Cruces Basin is filled with snow. Your old home is quiet. On the road below your house there are people rushing south, and I am grateful to have grown into a man with white in his beard. Thank you for the intervening years between the then and the now. Thank you for the wild places my mind recalls and my heart pounds out here, this letter, from your home, on a slight hill that looks east as the day burns itself to a black that is darker than blue.

Sincerely,
a.

An Open Letter on December 20th

The wounds were burning like suns
at five in the afternoon . . . Ah, that fatal five in the afternoon!
—*Federico Garcia Lorca*

december 20th
the setting sun has turned the sky to a color
i cannot describe
december 20th
a boy somewhere inside me
searches the llano for a borregero
the day is december 20th
the llano with its snow
is cold and white
on the 20th of december
a borregero
brings his flock home
on this day
women will come to screen doors
and wave at the passing borregero
it is december 20th
when i join in behind the herd
to hear a story of a horse so fast

on the 20th
by his arriving
the borregero defines home
Roger Arellano
rode a palomina horse
on december 20th 1979
today is december 20th 1997
and i wonder if that same horse

carries a borregero from this life
today the sky
is a bloodshot eye
or a face that has had too much wine

yesterday
i believed that clouds
painted in stained glass windows
it is the 20th of december
our borregero tells me of a horse so fast
it outran the rain
not every december is happy
not every memory of a borregero
is a good one
a borregero lives alone
and once a year
usually in december
Roger Arellano
on a day that wasn't the 20th of december
made me believe that stained glass clouds were sheep

a borregero lives alone
and once a year drinks too much wine
this is one of those unhappy decembers
every day of the year
including december 20th
a borregero smokes lucky strikes
a borregero dies in june
he is carried from this life on a fast horse
i learn of his death on december 20th
is any day
a good day to go to heaven

will the 20th suffice as well as the 19th
at this moment
i don't know if i'm a man or a boy

as a boy
during one of those good decembers
Roger lit a fire beneath a solitary cedar tree
still a borregero knows
that in the mind of children
it can always be a good december
today the sky
is an apple skin peeled with an old timer knife
no   this is still not right

on december 1st
these lonesome borregeros tell women they love
that they will be home on the 20th

in my boy's mind
i remember Roger Arellano
at my grandma's funeral
he asked my father for five dollars
he used it on wine
this was a bad december

on which winter night
did Roger Arellano shovel through a blizzard
only to find that come morning 23 sheep
ultimately in the december of your life
you will compare yourself
to an old wagon
i believe the day was
the 20th of december

Roger shoveled all night
but come morning
23 sheep died
in the deep snow drifts
the herd i walked behind
in december 1979
had 23 fewer sheep

december 1997
i imagine Roger's name
in the local paper
perhaps today
the sky is the color of heaven
reflecting off a glass of wine
are there calendars in heaven
does someone mark the date
when a man on the 20th of december remembers

i think of that horse almost every day
Roger told me that the rain fell
and the horse ran
the horse ran so fast
that on this day almost 20 years later
i still remember that only its tail got wet
not all memories
are as good as that one
maybe the sky is the color of an alcoholics skin

by all the calendars
it was december 20th
with the sun going down
Roger Arellano was his name

he told me once
i can't remember the day
that he saw two women skinny dipping

new mexico
that is where i am today
Roger told me
that they call it
the land of enchantment
because of those two women

not all memories are bad
just like not every december
is snowy
i used to be young
and i think that is my problem
today or any other
december 20th
and i am reminded
that i too am fading
toward that undefinable sky
this is why men
carve their names in trees
delaying their own decembers

Roger Arellano showed me a name
carved into a tree in 1933
no month was given
we used an old timer knife
the month was june
we carved our own names in that tree
i like the idea of my name growing
each letter stretching
a scar marking this and two other's lives

usually i do not feel so mortal
but today is december 20th
and my friend died the previous june
the sky to my left
on this 20th day of december
as i travel north
is the color of yesterday
today the herd is still on the llano
i search white hills
for our borregero his herd
i see neither

a borregero during a previous june
guides his herd home
he passes a tree with names carved in it
on that june day
i imagine Roger
rode the palomina horse
he had outlived
a borregeros name
grows on that tree
today is december 20th
a boy with curly hair
searches the llano for a borregero
on december 20th
that same boy looks again
as a man he sees nothing
a boy searched for a borregero
a man on the road home
searched for a borregero
on december 20th
he thought the sky looked like fire

It is Our Imperfections—Resilience

A Letter to the Headwaters from My River Dream,

Dear John,

It is good to be writing again; it has been too long. Since last we spoke I imagine you have seen many beautiful things and the world has opened up before you like fireworks on a dark and starless night; that must be the best kind of inspiration, the inspiration that comes from a place where passion and dedication meet in some powerful confluence with vision. Put another way my friend, the world has its heroes and some of them are blessed to do what they love, and some of them are double blessed to look upon a sacred mountain and know in that instant that they are the instrument of some greater good. I envy you for that, for the greater good you bring to the world, for your intelligence, and for your passion, but I am grateful too that there are people like you that defend our earth and our equally sacred, but somewhat more mundane, local and personal places. Anyway, I am writing you about this dream I've been having for a few years now, and like all my letters to the headwaters, there is always something that will not shake free from this web of mine.

It is my river dream, and in it there is only the smallest run of open water. The ice of the river has nearly come together, like a frozen and broken set of bones that will mend themselves whole in the short and brutal nights that January brings to my home. In my dream there are always different people there, at the lip of the water, and they are often young. I recognize them from the streets of my hometown. They are always alone at the edge of the ice, the black and nearly frozen water is the only moving thing there is. I can see it in their dream eyes, eyes brown as earth after a good and prolonged rain; each of them in their own version of the dream, is going to jump across the ice, and on the opposite shore there are willows juxtaposed red and almost glowing against all the white and ice. Because such things are clearer in dreams than they are in our waking moments, I know that the willows are the end of their life, that they will walk into the bosque on the far shore of that river, their dark clothes and thin bodies will ghost their way through the frozen fire of those willows and they will not come back.

I tell you this John without the proper context and apparently with little or no relation to the idea of Home/Land Security, our topic for this year's conference, and for the time it will take to make all those connections I must apologize. I have said it before and thus believe it to be true, there are four homes which need our protection, and I think that there are those among us that are masters at protecting whichever home we imagine to be the home most worth saving.

Some of them answer to the call of "now," the actual, persistent and present, home we all occupy, and for these champions there is always a calling, some new and important battle that needs their attention, some letter or phone conference that beckons them away from "real jobs" and the commitments that makes us human.

And there are those that protect our historical home because they know that from those roots there are innumerable sweet fruits that sustain us. They travel to places that have ruins of things ancient and things almost forgotten and they read the bones thrown by some prior hand, their divinations the key to knowing who we are now and who we might become. And there is the archetypal home, the one that I sometimes think of as the kingdom of elders and people with old and beautiful souls, the ones that persist where they should perish, the ones that rise daily from their beds of too many blankets and walk into their cold kitchens and begin the work of making a fire because that is what they have always done and that is what their mother and father did before them, and so on and so on and so on for generations without cease; they build the fire to a way of life that was and still is, the way life should be, the way, they presume, it was drawn up by the hand of God.

And what of our final home, the home of myth and legend, the place where memory and story exist, the home of our collective conscience, who is the keeper of that place? Some might argue that it is the writer's job to make such places live, to create from the well of myth and teach the reader the power of an old story, show them how they might find solutions to a modern world of problems in the godly workings of some deity or in the human actions of some selfless hero whose life has been elevated to myth by their courage and work. You see John, I do not deny that our places have these myths, these heroes, these legends of a shared and remembered past. There are countless books dedicated to just such people, and I do not believe it necessary to pursue such mythological champions further.

Rather, I wish to discuss with you the overlooked place of myth, the four chambered homeland that is our human heart and the brave battle that the poor fight on a daily basis to protect their last and only defensible homeland from a world that sees them as lazy, shiftless, and without light. The heart, at the risk of nearing the hilt of cliché, is the place where all the greatest myths persist. These myths, which to some are actual and attainable dreams that can be realized through good fortune, being born right or in the rare case by someone that is willing to work their tiredness into something great. But for others the myths of the heart, the mythical homeland and the genesis of hope is simply the stuff of wish and want, illusory dreams of equality, equity, and the old lie of "liberty and justice for all." These myths are the uncatchable fire that burns as it recedes, the Tantalus and Sisyphus that Countee Cullen spoke of.

In my dream the icy edges of the river are populated by the ghosts of my hometown, the ones I, perhaps, too often write about. Perhaps it was too much Neruda too soon, the Juan Coldeater, the Juan Barefoot and the Juan Stonecutter of Macchu Picchu whose lives he lends his voice to and whose anonymous lives lend their unending influence over me.

And so I wonder who will be the keeper of the fierce and clawed myths of the poor, those of the human heart, those that have at their core a semblance of hope, a hope that fires the human engine even as it drains it, a hope like vines itself to a notion that things will get better despite the obvious signs to the contrary.

James Baldwin called it the Myth of America, and while I love my country I hold no illusions about the poverty I see on a daily basis and those sentinels that guard their hearts with the fierceness of stoic warriors without weapons, shields or a discernible code, warriors whose only recourse is their anger and whatever demon they use to satiate and extinguish the larger demon of their assimilation and emasculation. What gifts might they now offer the world had their land not been stolen over a century before their birth? What great strength might they exude there upon their corner among the bottles, anger and lingering smoke had they first been given an actual home they could love rather than resent?

You see John, I see these doppelgangers, watch their frail shadows move upon the crumbling walls of my town, see the shuffle of feet upon the sidewalks, roads and parking lots that have known their every fall, and I think I know what it is their heart might be feeling. I feel it myself at times, and while I do not intend for this letter to be about me, know that I am a giving soul, a fixer, a coach, a confirmation teacher, a professor, a parish council president, a community activist, a campus activist, a youth group leader, a father and a husband, a human breathing and feeling being that knows the despair of action met with complacency, selflessness met with avarice and joy met with loss, and I understand how it is that love, that highest of human potentials, can find a way to protect itself amongst the thorns of poverty and apathy.

Luis Valdez' Pachuco urged Henry Reyna to "wrap his loves in hate," and that seems to make so little sense until you see what it is that is truly loved and how much of what was previously loved has gone away. What, at first, seems counterintuitive, the yards left to decay and neglect, the broken windows of town, the walls tagged with the scrawl of pseudo-ownership, the abandoned houses gutted by fire or taxes that could not be paid, the teenager lost upon the midnight streets, the middle aged man still reliving that ancient wrestling match where he pinned his opponent, all of it is the work of warriors, broken men and women whose only unbroken parts are the myths they hold to in their fortress of a heart, warriors that in their own way and in the absence of language, heritage, culture and money, protect their home/land by the only means left them.

A passing traveler may look upon the meadows that surround Antonito, find their gaze captured by the diamond glint of the rivers, or feel themselves lifted by the peaks that ring us, and undoubtedly they must say to themselves "beautiful, just beautiful." Those with the means have already begun to buy up every canyon, and others have begun their buy-out of the ranches and bottom land. But the town itself, like a broken and tattered heart of a home, still stands largely ignored, its poor and fierce looking warriors standing their perpetual guard over all that remains of what they previously loved, that which their original and ancient heart tells them used to be precious.

In my river dream, the ribs of ice are almost fused together and there is a ribbon of black water that flows toward the east; and there is always some forgotten but committed warrior waiting to leap toward the red willows directly across from him. In the dream he leaps high into the morning air and he sails higher than is possible anywhere but in dreams. His eyes are clear. Below him he sees the near dormant fish finning near the black and round stones of the riverbed. And in my dream there is a woman singing, a mother's voice, her notes of joy and grief linger there together with the eerie harmony of her son's leap. The blackbirds at the water's edge look up and take flight. The world is made of sky. The trees have bloomed green like trees blooming green in spring and the song's lyrics are as clear as the memory of a first love. I think you know the song, my friend, the song which tells us there is no home, no land, no security, none of it, until these forgotten, these broken Juan Coldeaters, Juan Barefoots, and Juan Stonecutters, nothing at all, not even a dream of peace or security, until these stooped sentinels are cared for, until someone loves them with the very same fierceness they exude.

John, despite all appearances to the contrary, I do believe that my dream ends happily. Always, before I wake, the people of my dream turn away from the red willows, and though I cannot say for certain where they go, they do, in fact, walk off in the direction of home, toward the fires that have just now begun to breathe sweet wood smoke into the day.

Here's to, as always, wishing you a secure home and land, one that prospers and is made whole by whichever of its four chambers we find ourselves protecting. That is my wish, and it too is a dream.

Much peace,

a.

A Letter to Mumper from a 4:00 a.m. Campus

Dear Michael,

Only the deer welcome me to campus,
quiet as question marks they lift their heads
and watch me as i move toward the building. They are not like the deer
i have known all my life. There is no fear in their bodies,
no tensed muscles locked and set on the edge of
some real or imagined flight from danger.
They graze in the thick fog, in the memory of yesterday's rain
as it lingers and kisses at the lights of campus; they graze as everything glows
new and ghostly. None of them seem to dream of running; they seem
to have some other purpose that is not immediately evident.
The smallest of the bunch steps toward me, a young doe,
her eyes are dark planets, legs as thin as razors of bone and flesh.

My first year at Adams i met Raynell Gallegos. She was in my
Comm Arts I class, sitting at the back of the room. She had long hair
in tight curls, thin rays of blonde highlights rivered through
and disappeared as they neared her shoulders. Her eyes were dark and round.
She smiled often. I believe that she loved school, our school, the promise of it.
She would ask me about various paper topics, if i believed they
were good. i was an adjunct, newly married and working for $2900 per section,
but she trusted me when i told her that i did not believe she was writing about
her true subjects. She looked at me, there was questioning in her eyes,
but she nodded and moved toward her desk; her pen pushing
furiously at the paper as she purged some truer subject from everything she
had ever been told about writing. She confided in me, told me how her other
    professors
said her writing was unorganized and lacked clarity. i believe we understood
one another, she from San Luis, me from Antonito. We knew in our
collective memory, the way so many of our students know,

that really, despite the slogans, mission statements and
educated people around us that profess our place in the academic world,
that really, in the true place the heart cannot reveal, a stored place for secrets,
wishes and fear, both of us felt like we did not belong.

i assured Raynell that her writing was as circular and ancient as
moons, planets and suns, her thoughts looping toward one another in
intersecting orbits of joy, pain, and hope, each sentence linked by
some invisible yet obvious confluence with her language,
oral tradition, heritage, ancestors and unique worldview.

i did not know it then, but in retrospect i think she knew
that she was dying, that there was a tumor in her brain, draining daily
everything that she had ever known and smiled at.
i believe now, nearly 15 years later, that she considered the possibility
that education could literally save her life, how there is
magic in books, defined and catalogued magic, indexed, annotated and given
to us for the sole purpose of making us beautiful and whole.

That is a tall order, for all of us, to save lives with our knowledge
to provide hope where hope is sometimes as limited as sight in a dark
    windowless room.

Raynell, disappeared after that, not in the literal sense that death brings,
though she did pass some years later. Some hand
pulled her away from school, from her vision of
who she wanted to be. It may have been something
as dire and simple as her failing health
that took her away from school, but i have been here long enough,
seen my share of the young ghosts whose dream
has been snuffed out by some unwritten code the faculty, too often, follow.

(i know that is cliché, but it is a dream, the moments
where we imagine ourselves better than we started, more intelligent and grown)

i love Adams State, want her to prosper, but i too have taken part in the
unintentional and sometimes subliminal derailing of students,
participated in the expectation that, somehow, they are subpar,
that perhaps we are also subpar because this is where we "settled".
i hear my colleagues in meetings, in the hallway, in social gatherings,
sometimes in our silence, lamenting the quality of our students,
perhaps secretly wishing that we were at a better or bigger school or both.
We find, in the midst of those conversations, our diamonds,
the ones we hold up to the others as examples
of what is possible, our few and gleaming examples of
intelligent students, the ones that slake our thirst and supposedly keep us.

Lately, i have come to this revelation, like salvation
finally visited upon the sinner, just how brilliant and powerful
our students really are. We seek out the diamonds, the ones
that are most like us and for them the world is opened,
the magic loosed upon them in a supernova of knowledge
and the newly minted hope that all learning delivers. Yet,
for those that are not like us, the ones that have not
"done their best work" or "not tried hard enough" . . . those
students, they are the ones we hold up as
what is wrong with Adams State.

i remember a faculty meeting, my first year here. As an
adjunct i did not dare speak up when my colleagues
began discussing the inadequacies of Raynell and her writing.
One of them asked who her Comm Arts teacher was, and i
did not raise my hand, i was silent as 4:00 a.m. deer. Later,
the same professor came to my office and chastised me
for passing her, with an "A", no less. Apparently,
Raynell had told this professor that "Mr. Abeyta said this
was good writing".

Years later, i am sure she was wearing a wig, but i did
not dare ask. i, once again, saw Raynell in the hallway. She had decided
to come back to school. She was nice to me; we spoke for a few
minutes and she revealed that she had been very sick but was
feeling better now.

i think of Raynell more often now, i can no longer
hear her real voice, only this one that asked to be included in
this letter to you, only this one that i have adopted here; it is a
soft voice. You may need to strain in order to hear it among the louder
voices of celebration, exuberance and growth.

i cannot say for certain why she comes to me
on these a.m. walks, in the short distance
between my vehicle and the door to the building. Perhaps
this is her earthly place, not a haunting, her voice
is at peace, but rather a place for her to rest from the
work of an afterlife, the constant prayers of family

the business of being diligent for us that do not
pay enough attention.

i am not saying that Raynell was a great student
but i believe she had faith in the power of education,
faith in what is, for some, the slow and arduous steamroller
of learning that lays low the many obstacles placed in
their paths, the obstacle of illness, of poverty
of schools that never believe, the obstacle of family obligations,
obstacles of hunger both literal and figurative; obstacles of devastated
homes ruined by divorce or shattered by violence
the obstacles of low expectations, of broken and weary bodies,
of unanswered prayers, of fallen friends, of wells that go dry, and jail doors
      that close,

obstacles of bottles that drain daily like an intravenous prayer for hope,
drugs that evaporate into blood for generations,
fields that call for plow and shovel, animals that need tending,
a child that needs someone to see her play,
all of this is the miracle of what Adams State does, a magic of joy,
sweat and perseverance that makes our students
the best in the country. Each of them, in their own way,
despite their obstacles has come here for a sole purpose,
to be better. They are strong as memory, strong as blood,
strong as a valley wind, each a constellation of their many parts,
some stars brighter, others red and dying, all of them constant
in their burning.

Soon, the voices of students will reverberate down the halls
and sidewalks as they move, seemingly without effort,
toward their classrooms and the professors they may come to trust.
None of us shall see their load, the invisible weight they carry,
the heaviness that has made them strong.

The planet eyed doe takes another step in my direction,
she turns toward the other deer, all of them watching
as i enter the building, ears set on edge as if i might
possibly speak to them. i nod in their direction, almost wave
as if something invisible has commanded it; they disappear
into the fog, only a memory of their sleek bodies and dark
eyes lingers; the door clicks behind me, the building is empty,
Raynell and the others like her finally let go and
leave me to my work.

much peace,
a.

116

A letter to the Men of Troy Concerning the Nature of Joy

Dear Men,

I've considered this letter for some time now, the details of it, the relative truth of it, whether there is credence in what I am about to tell you. Many thoughts kite their way in and out of the valleys and rifts of my mind. It is, after all, just a football game, played out on a field with boys and young men as the architects of loss and victory. That is what is beautiful about football, the basic and uncompromised simplicity of it; force on force, and often times the laws of physics do prevail. It is those moments, the ones away from the field, away from practice, away from your demanding coaches and the vicarious wishes of your community, parents and school, where the laws of physics do not apply, not in the traditional sense anyway. Sir Isaac Newton says that for every action there is an equal and opposite reaction and that gravity, regardless of the weight of the object, is consistent for two falling objects. I honestly do not believe this is true for our community, for our team, for the relatively short span of your lives thus far.

Gravity is not something that is consistent for us; there are many un-weighed and invisible things in the scale, heavy things, leaden and dead in their push, their burden which your young legs have been left to carry. For whatever reason, the people of Antonito seem to fall faster and rise slower than their less burdened neighbors. I'm not trying to make victims of our people; we are strong, all of us, in our resistance, our persistence, our perseverance. I've said it before. The people of Antonito live, and I mean live in the truest sense of the word, through this team. You represent for them the ability to overcome the yoke of oppression and failure. It is amazing what gifts and responsibilities have been left to the hearts of our young warriors, you, the Men of Troy. You prove to your community, every time you take the field, that the force of a bigger opponent is not equal to your will, that their size cannot equally and oppositely effect your determination. I believe, in every moment of my existence and with every

117

fiber of my body, that the soul of this team is unconquerable. Perhaps it is naïve of me to say this, but I believe that football is the only sport where physics, where the laws of how things do and should work, do not apply. For decades this team was invisible. You have made us visible. You have, even when defeat has placed its heavy hand upon your shoulder, represented hope. You, Men of Troy, are the personifications of joy.

So I suppose that is what I really want to talk about, joy. It does not seem like a word that football players should use, and certainly not their coach. Joy is a word reserved for children, the innocent, the uninitiated few who have not felt the pull and anchor of a gravity that is palpable and real, the gravity which is life in a poor community. Joy is reserved for the rich. Joy is something that lives somewhere else. Joy cannot coexist with the callused hands and bowed backs of the people you love. Life is a constant struggle. Survival always trumps joy. These are the definitions I grew up with, the ones I carry like a library of broken things written into every book and every person I have had the pleasure of knowing, caring for and loving.

I am, by nature, a positive person. Happy. Joyful. Yet I looked at my players last Friday night, as they watched Sanford play Sierra Grande. I watched as Sanford's quarterback yelled, whooped and postured every time his team made a good play. I watched as each of your eyes turned to the referees, waiting, as if knowing in some deep core where knowing is innate and unspoken, for the yellow flag to come. Once, twice, three times. We all watched and the flag did not come. That is when one of you said it, what all of us were thinking. "We would have gotten a penalty the first time." I believe this to be true. I cannot say if that player's joy was legitimate or forced, perhaps both, but I know that we are not afforded that same joy. It is not allowed, both literally and figuratively, because we would be transcending the place, the low and grounded place their mind has always placed us in. An Antonito team that wins is a team that does not fit their perception of how things should be. Even after two winning seasons, each of us knows that we are not given the respect you deserve.

I grew up hearing something. It was not pleasant, and it had many variations, but the general idea never wavered. "Eventually Antonito will beat themselves," "they get too emotional and forget how to play," "they will self-destruct," "they just don't know how to win," "they got lucky," "we just overlooked them," "they don't know how to play as a team." The list seems infinite now as I recount them. I was in school 21 years ago. I'm willing to bet that each of you has heard similar things, even today. These comments are not variations of any truth. They are all variations of how people have viewed us for generations. It's not that you are now allowed to win in their minds. It's that you are not allowed to change the way they view you.

I had a long talk with Sanford's principal last week. I bet each of you can guess where the conversation led. Whose tone was meant to put the other in his place, whose words were meant to dictate who was in charge. I am so used to this bullshit; it doesn't even bother me anymore. I put it in my file, my book of wrongs, my thick and heavy book of motivation and I go there, not for vengeance or some other form of pay-back. I go there for strength. We are all from the same place. We all have different lives. Yet, I will venture to say that we all have that same book, that same list of memories where our joy was not allowed or disavowed as false, fleeting or lucky. None of you are false, fleeting or lucky. Each of you is real, permanent, and it is your hard work that brought you here.

So what does all of this have to do with joy, with football, with a game? There are very few moments in life that our heart and brain agree upon, the moments that our being and memory make permanent. I used to believe that these moments of permanence were part of the natural state of living: marriages, funerals, the indelible memories of falling in love; I thought permanent things were concrete things. I know now that hard work, perseverance, brotherhood, athleticism and teamwork are capable of making even the abstract permanent. A parent told me recently, while recounting last year's game, that he "could die happy" because he had now lived to see the day when Antonito beat Sanford on the football field. I guarantee you that the players from Sanford viewed that loss as a fluke, Antonito lucking out. They are sure in their long held stance that, eventually, because it always does, the gravity of Antonito's past will pull their teams back down to where they belong. Your coaches have not been teaching you how to play football. It is simply our vehicle to teach you how to live correctly, to always rise, to bring a much deserved joy to a people, place, school and community that haven't experienced it enough. It is just a game and it is more than a game. It is a battle for something permanent and lasting. Both teams are playing for something much larger than a final score. Sanford is playing for things to return to the way they used to be. You are playing for all of your hard work to be made manifest, made completely real, no longer written off as simply a fluke or oversight on the other team's part. You are playing for the joy of knowing something permanent. You are young, not responsible for what has happened in the past. You are only the agents of a new Antonito, agents of change, where joy is expected, deserved, and permanent.

I've said it before. Your coaches love each of you. We believe, completely, in all of you. Now comes the hard part, the part where you accept that you have earned the right to be great, to defy the laws of physics in a very human way. You have earned the right to leave any field as champions. We simply need to know that about ourselves and not let the devils of doubt and dissent enter into our consciousness. Know that you are great. Know that joy is yours and is permanent. Know that the Men of Troy took the field this season, not as the beneficiaries of a supposedly "better" team last year, but as the rightful heirs of a new tradition, one that we are obligated and completely capable of upholding. Winning.

God Bless & God Speed Men of Troy.

A Letter to the Men of Troy

Dear Team,

As you read this letter you must know that in less than 24 hours you will face an opponent who means to do you harm. This letter is not to recount what you already know. This letter is my wish for all of you. It is the wish of all your coaches and the wish of your community. Simply put, everyone that cares for you is wishing for your success. Please understand that this success has very little to do with the football field and is, in fact, more a case of where your life will lead. What you do on the field tomorrow and every time you take the field will be a metaphor, a symbol of sorts, for how you will lead your life. You may not realize this now, but I assure you that life will deal you harder blows than any opponent ever will. How you react to adversity, to being knocked down will be the measure of your character.

I am reminded, as I write this, of a quote by Dr. Martin Luther King Jr. He said, "It is always difficult to get out of Egypt. The Red Sea always looms before you with discouraging dimensions." He, of course, was not referring to football, but instead to a human struggle within all of us, a struggle to know your own worth and to be allowed to display that worth to the world. Rest assured that I, and your coaches, have taken measure of your worth and we know that you are the finest group of young men to ever take this field, bar none. Even so, there is still the matter of the Red Sea that stood between Moses and the freedom of his people, freedom from Pharaoh's slavery.

Gentlemen, all of us, at some point in our lives, will be slaves to something which appears greater than us. For this team, I offer that we are slaves to doubt and slaves to a culture of loss. Our Red Sea is the overwhelming expectation that you will lose, because you have never won. Your Red Sea is your classmate that mocks you and tells you, without knowing your sacrifice, without knowing your heart, that you will lose in your new jerseys same as you did in your old ones. Your Red Sea, your escape from Egypt, will always be the teachers and coaches who have no faith in you; they will manifest this lack of faith by not pushing you to be better. They will expect simply what they offer you, nothing. They will not teach you math because they expect that such a skill will not be relevant to a Mexican kid from Antonito. You will have coaches that believe you cannot learn plays because, after all, "they're not even smart enough to pass English, how can you expect them to learn 40 plays."

Your Egypt will always be a difficult place to escape from. Your opponent tomorrow will appear to you, perhaps, like the Red Sea appeared to Moses and his people, insurmountable; that sea parted and Pharaoh's army pursued them intent on never letting any of them be free. Pharaoh's army, for us, is the doubt that pursues us and seeks to always keep us, the doubt that depends on failure for its food. Doubt is the creation of someone who has not succeeded. They will, if you let them, seek to place their failures on your shoulders. They will, only if you let them, tell you how easy it is to lose. I promise you, winning will be the most difficult thing you ever do, but it will be the only thing you will point to many years from now. Winning will feel like pain and losing will always feel like lying down. The person who heaps doubt and a culture of loss in your direction will tell you, always, how big the other team is, they will tell you how hard you tried, they will tell you that you played well and your teammates did not, they will tell you that you should come out with them and party because you're going to lose anyway, they will tell you lying down is easy because that is what they know. The doubter will not have risen in the pre-dawn of morning to make a 5:30 a.m. practice. The doubter will not have, for their brother, sacrificed sleep and comfort so that his friends and teammates can make it to work on time. The doubter will not have run beside you and pushed you when you felt as though your lungs and legs were ready to explode. The doubter will not have seen the early morning sun rise above your home and burn away the dew from your field. May that sun, with its rising, be a symbol for you. May the early sun burn away the chill of loss from your bodies, may it burn away the dew of doubt that clung to your clothes and every limb. May that orange hue, as it crept over the horizon, be your reminder of strength. May it remind you that all of your opponents are the Red Sea and may your strength and brotherhood always be its parting.

Tomorrow, a new Trojan team will take the field; make this your warrant: When you are tired, rise. When you have fallen, rise. When your opponent has knocked you down, always rise. Rise for the brother next to you. Rise for the people that love you. Rise, always for your school and community, but most important of all, rise for yourself so that you may be measured and counted as a man, one of many men that is your team and therefore your family, The Men of Troy.

A Letter to Guillermo, Having Missed His Call

dear Guillermo

i have been waiting for just such an occasion to write you, a good snow, the flakes fat and wet, the earth silent. My wish is that you are well and writing long poems with words like drums.

South and east of me the sky is the color of smoke from a house burning in autumn. If a person could get past the image of the man in the gray jacket, his pants rolled above his work boots, past the image of the man shaking his head, it would be quite beautiful this sky and that burning house.

i want you to know that i appreciated the call from you and Cynthia. i was sorry to have missed it though i cannot say that i would have been one for talking. i feel better now about all that has happened. At some point, there was a part of me, with my abuelito, that took its final breath at 1:35 p.m. on February 15th, a deep final breath as though we were both intending to go under water.

i miss my abuelito find great comfort in Walt Whitman who believed that every soul was beautiful, that the soul was always beautiful. i can see now why you said you would want him to lead you through Dante's inferno, though i do not wish fire for anyone, especially that man shaking his head at the beginning of this letter.

It is now 9:17 p.m., the sky is entirely black, the moon and stars have no address in our southern sky, though i am sure that Orion is still out there tilted in the west hunting through the sky. In a few months he will go to his summer home in another hemisphere.

i must be more observant and take note of my friends more often, those real like yourself and those cold and untouchable miles upon miles away in the sky. By now you have probably grown tired of me mentioning Venus to you and in relation to you but you must know, as i do, that she is blazing in the west in the early evenings, though tonight she rested somewhere behind snow filled clouds.

Michele is improving from her long month. Everyone has noticed a color in her skin that was not there before. We that love her and are around her every day did not see summer leave her face and we realize that we were not observant enough. i have made a vow to be more observant, to remember better, people at their best.

Michele too was happy to hear from you and Cynthia and has relayed to me the subtleties of your voices and what they meant. She says her thanks through these words and i write them for her.

The snow returns like the march snows i used to pray for, the very same snow my brother and i would work in as we fed the sheep. My brother, left handed Andrew, is sad now without our abuelito. His cries of my grandpa, my grandpa and his tears that betrayed him, the fighter, are still haunting me.

i always knew that my abuelito loved him best, that Andrew loved him best, but i cannot bring myself to see my brother sad in the eyes.

My abuelito's house is empty now. "Tonight I can write the saddest lines," makes even more sense now. Do i always write to you with sadness in my voice?

Well Guillermo, i will say goodbye for now as the stereo plays its last song, something about pretty lies.

The snow is good for me. i will watch it until sleep comes or until it turns itself to cloud and moves like smoke over the Sangre de Cristos. Do you think that the snow is always beautiful, that all snow is beautiful, that Whitman might think it to be like the souls in Leaves of Grass?

> Goodnight amigo, stay warm.
> adios, a.

A Letter to the Antonito High School Graduating Class of 2013 Regarding Their Book of Dreams, Happiness and Other Perpetual Things

Dear Graduates,

I want to thank you for inviting me to speak tonight; it is my honor and privilege to do so. Twenty-Four years ago I sat in approximately the same place you are sitting tonight, and in that moment I was completely sure where my life would lead. I had made plans, an escape route away from Antonito, past the landmines of doubt, fear and pain that I believed kept people living here. Despite my presumed knowledge, I soon learned that everything I believed to be true was only a shadow of what really was. I learned, because that is what we all must do; we all must continue learning and by doing so bring light to the dark places of our human soul. It is this very light that makes us see more clearly the joy and grace of where we are from. Let me get this out of the way, so that there is no doubt. You are graduates of the best school I have ever attended. Through fate, through misguided pride and through the pursuit of my education I went to school in three different districts and attended two different universities and now teach kids from all over the world, and though I am biased, I assure you that there is no better school than the one we are in tonight. I am biased not because I am from Antonito and I need to represent. I am predisposed to feel this way because I know that it was this place, these people, this town, and this school that sustained me, always, even when the world was bleak as a moonless and starless night; Antonito glowed in my memory, as if my soul was cresting the hill near San Antonio Mountain and looked upon our home in the lonely night, appearing there against the night, the orange and white embers of the lights of town filled my heart and made me whole again; my soul was a traveler that always returned home. We are all blessed that this is our home and that this is our school.

So what will come after this night? Where will you travel to after you venture out into the world? What will you write in your book of dreams? What new chapters will be added after this ceremony? What new characters will grace the pages of the novel you have been writing for the past twelve years?

Will the hero in your book of dreams look like you? Will the main character bleed blood that has coursed through this community for nearly 200 years? Will your book echo of a small town life and friends you will greet for the rest of your life? What will be in your book of dreams, will the hero fly over the broken things of this place and see where his or her hand can mend what has fallen? Will the hero in this book, your book of dreams, seek out that that perfect note, that dream of music that lives and prospers where no on can ever touch it, the immortal place in each of you that persists where it should perish, survives where it should stumble and thrives where it should wither? And will your hero be sustained by a perfect note of music, a guitar of hope straining, but with grace and perseverance, against what is broken? Will your hero, this person that looks and acts like you, be kissed awake by the grace of their own strength and the melody of that straining guitar, and will their heart be made full, to give and to give, and to give of that perfection? Will your hero, the one in your book of dreams, change the landscape of the world with his or her love?

Because that is the paradox of this place, the beautiful and haunting harmony no outsider will ever understand; we, as a people, give to each other and from ourselves what is left to us, our deep love, the deep and grace filled note of music which stands in for our souls at times, fills our hearts, fills our bellies, and fills our ancient and immovable sense of community. We give to each other this grace. We give to one another what can only be called love; it is our last and unbroken treasure, and it is present in each of you. It lives upon your smiles and in your unfaltering spirit.

I believe God has placed it there, having first bestowed it upon your ancestors many generations ago. Imagine this place back then, an open wilderness with no connection to an outside world beyond where their eyes could reach up to; there, against the horizon, was the end of their world. What did they have? Surely, there was not money. There could not have been much of anything for them to rely upon except each other. The same fortitude that allowed them to survive and grow to love one another is not something that geneticists can trace or map, but I assure you that it is there, like uncut diamonds of longing, hope and strength; the very same diamonds glow within you, this beautiful class of graduates, like a fire of knowledge and persistence. The strength of these heroes that came before you, to this day, nourishes and nurtures each and every one of us, whispers of our culture, heritage, strength and beauty. Do not ever forget them. Write them into your book. Write their story so that the harsh and fast world will know of the high and alpine place where your dreams were born and by knowing understand that those dreams are as sacred as human life and therefore must be left within you, not stripped away like the garments of language, culture, community and virtue that the outside world calls assimilation and standardization. In short, never forget where you come from and that you are ancient, strong and beautiful.

You alone are the author of the chapters that follow. The philosopher, Plato, theorized that what all humans had in common was their desire to be happy and that their happiness was a direct consequence of a healthy soul. So for you, regardless of what you write into your book, I wish for each of you a healthy soul, one of your own making and one constructed and filled with joy. This is no small thing, what I am suggesting, that you alone are the arbiters of your own happiness; you must be both the bucket and the cool sweet water that fills and refills your human soul. Though I wish you happiness and joy, none of us are that naïve. There will be pain, loneliness, despair, and failure; the book never turns out the way we anticipated. There are complications, reversals, and knots that tighten and loosen and some that break altogether. So tonight, as you embark on the voyage of the rest of your life, I offer that happiness is not something that you can draw a plan for; there is no formula, no map or compass that points us in the right direction, no fixed star to guide us through a night of despair and pain toward the safe harbor of happiness. Rather, it is happiness that will find you, but you must call out to it, you must summon it from the forest of doubts, from the islands of loneliness, dream it from the open fields of your mind; you must always call out to it so that it knows your voice. Doubt is the devil's work, but silence is his reward. You must sing out. You must always raise your voice; it is your duty to sing, to always sing so that happiness can find you and rest its grace upon you.

Remember this though, when happiness fills your soul, remember that this work of being happy is not, nor has it ever been a selfish endeavor. You must come back to the people that cannot call out any longer, the ones whose voice has been cut away by the knife of poverty, despair, and the daily task of living. You must sing for the ones that cannot sing; that is what we, as a people, have always done, and it is what we must continue doing. It is written in a book somewhere, and you should write it in your own book.

As you write your book of dreams, please remember where you came from and what you accomplished there. Remember your town that sometimes camouflages its love, beauty and strength with broken bottles and buildings as vacant as lost souls. Remember your school and the memories of the pages you wrote here.

And remember this; do not back away from the villains that come to live in your book of dreams. They are as necessary as faith for they will test your resolve, and it is their attempted fashioning that will instead carve you into an even stronger person. You must never let the idiots win. Do not listen to their whispers of doubt as a substitute for truth. Do not heed the assertions where they tell you that you are poor, that your school is dying, that your place is broken. The villain in your book will tell you of better things and places, how salvation, power and success are beyond this place. That is the work of the bad guy in every book; their benevolence is always self-serving and hollow.

Never forget that each of you is like that light that glows in the dark of night and covers and warms this town with its embers. Each of you is the light, the hope and the voice that can mend us and make us whole. The poet, Yeats, said that with dreams begin responsibilities and perhaps I am asking and expecting too much of you, but I see in this class something which is great and cannot be taught. Perhaps the dreams written into your book are the beginning of your responsibilities, your adult and human responsibility to lead, not for the sake of power or forced ego, but to lead because that is what your heart is conditioned to do. Each of you is capable of being a leader, each of you capable of changing the world, of building something lasting and beautiful, constructing from light, song and your human voice what your community knows is possible, that each of you is the hero in this book of yours, the hero that returns, because that is what heroes do; they return to our longing ears as a beautifully struck note of music. You are the hero, the guitar of hope and the singing voice. This dozen, this beautiful group of classmates and friends can be the voice that sings us whole, reaches us and sings us whole, the light that mends what is broken, the light that enters through the broken parts of us as well as the broken parts of this town. You, dear graduates are the light, the voice, the hero that mends us whole.

God Bless and God Speed Graduates, may happiness find you and may your song, like your school and hometown, live forever.

Much Peace,

a.

A Letter to the Men of Troy, Where I Explain A Few Things

Dear Team,

I suppose there are several reasons why I get to the field so early, reasons why I get out of my truck and, as if by instinct, walk toward the north end zone. It is how I do my penance, why I coach and why I love each of you. Let me explain.

I have always been the first one to the field; it's my thing. Even when I played I took pride in beating the coaches to practice, but that's not why I coach. My reasons for that are complicated and not easily defined, but the simplest way to explain it would be to tell you about the second guy to practice. I won't mention his name because I don't want to hurt his family, or perhaps it just hurts me a bit too much to mention his name. I will call him X, and he was a good guy, a year ahead of me in school. He wouldn't get to practice early to warm up, throw the ball or put his pads on. He would get to practice early so he could smoke before the coaches arrived. Everyone on the team knew what he was doing and we made jokes about his glazed eyes and how he would mask the smell with cigarette smoke. He always parked at the north end of the field. I never suspected that he might be in pain or that he needed or lacked for anything; truth be told, he may have been perfectly okay. The real issue was that I did nothing. I'm not talking about snitching or some elaborate knight in shining armor bullshit. I simply did nothing, absolutely nothing and a year or so later he had taken his own life.

I'm not telling you this as a means to forgiveness or as some forgotten or belated apology. I'm simply telling you all of this because sometimes football and life intersect in imperceptible yet powerful ways.

All season your coaches have asked you to be perfect. We have yelled, asked nicely, shown and explained and in terms of wins and losses you have been perfect. But I guess we are all looking for something bigger; all of you too are looking for this very same thing.

The other day as I was walking toward the north end zone to offer my regards and apologies to X, it occurred to me why this team is so great and why it is that we push you so hard. I've been under the misconception all season that the Sanfords, La Vetas, Granadas, Elberts, Daysprings and Merinos were the opponent. I couldn't have been more wrong. We are perfect and we strive for perfection, not because of some ideal image of what a champion should be, but because of the opponents we overcome on a daily basis. Put another way, it is our imperfections, our struggles, our daily lives, that make this team amazing and therefore perfect.

We are a family, all of us connected in ways that extend beyond city limits, school walls, team pride and cheering fans. If you have ever come home to a dinner of plain rice and beans because there wasn't anything else, then you have already beaten Granada. If the lights and the phone have been shut off because there was no money left to pay for those things then you have already beaten Elbert or Sanford, if you've come home to a yard of weeds and packed earth, you've already beaten Merino. If you've ever wallowed in a jail cell removed from real light and air and your only wish was a simple one, to run and run and stop at your heart's content then you have already beaten Dayspring. If you have broken bones and waited a long year to join your family on the field, if you have pissed blood and waited for your kidneys to work, if you have ever lost brothers, sisters or children, if you have ever been abandoned by your family, buried a family member before their time, found solace in a bottle or a joint, helped your drunken friends or family members to bed, watched your friends and classmates disappear from your life and into the oblivion of drugs, alcohol and dropout status, if you have ever been cast into fatherhood before you were ready and if you have ever been made to piss in a cup to prove your worth, if you have ever sat invisible, unknown, and uncared for in a classroom, if you have ever stayed up into the thin hours of night waiting for your brother or father to come home, if you have never really known your father or mother and if you have ever been called a dirty Mexican or made to fear that everyone you love could be sent away on the whim of a politician or police officer, if you have ever been called a loser or quitter, if you have ever found yourself wishing that people wouldn't drink so much, or if you have suffered through the desert of divorce and betrayal, if you have fallen away from your heritage and language, if you have ever been made to feel inferior, or if you have ever had your heart broken, or tasted defeat in the shadow of a corn field in eastern Colorado, or suffered through an interminable night in a place in the middle of the Big Gypsum Valley where three of your brothers were sent to the hospital, if you have suffered through any or many of these, if you have borne the burdens of grown men and women before your time, then you have already won. You are perfect, not because you beat other teams on the gridiron, you are perfect because your imperfections have not beaten you. Your opponents for the next four weeks are these little blips on the radar of what you have already overcome and all that you have defeated.

I'm not saying that the games will be easy simply because of your hardships. The world is full of people who live in their own lament, convinced that theirs is the only tragedy on earth. I know this is not any of you. Each of you is brave beyond words and the guy lined up across from you each week and for the rest of your life is your opportunity to show your courage, to let your imperfections feed your perfection.

Many of you will never come this way again. Football and success are fleeting, and I can assure you of several things. It is the lie of a broken dream that is hardest to forget, and it is the things you loved in vain because you did not do them that stay with you like a tattoo of regret. I wish I would have been wiser, twenty years ago, when I stepped onto our field. But I suppose wisdom is not meant entirely for the young. Instead, you have been given strength, speed, deep and powerful hearts, you have been given each other, family on every side of you. It's true, I believe in God and I believe in blessings. I truly believe that we have been blessed, not with football prowess, though we have that, not with the cheers of our community, though we have that too. Our blessings are less tangible and measurable than all of that. It won't be found on the scoreboard or stat sheet. Eventually those numbers will fade and exact scores and yards gained will disappear like smoke in the wind. What will last is how this team, a band of brothers and one brave sister approached the great opponents of doubt and imperfection and came away unbeaten, stronger for their failings and their weaknesses.

A favorite poet of mine says that "hope is a thing with feathers" and she may be right, but for me, hope is a thing with deep roots of pain, regret, loss, hardship, and struggle. It is 33 men and one woman that board the bus or take the field with one goal, to be there for each other, to coach and play for each other and leave nothing in doubt, that their greatness will be known for generations.

They will say that this group was perfect, that this group was undefeated, but they will not know what we know, that "the world breaks everyone and afterward many are stronger in the broken places." The quote does not say that all are stronger; it only promises that many are. We are only a few, but we are all stronger in the broken places. Perfect because we play for one another, perfect and undefeated long before the game commences, perfect long before your coach gets to an empty field and paces north toward his ghosts, toward the end zone and a giant rock that marks our strength. We were perfect long ago, before the record, the scoreboard or the paper said it was so, and now we have been blessed with the opportunity to prove ourselves.

There are four teams and thirty two opponents in your way. May each of them know what I and your coaches know. Champions live and play here, on the fields of Troy, here on the high llano of our home, here surrounded by the broken things and the fallen things. May they know that we are made perfect despite the broken and fallen things. May they know that champions took the field one autumn and drew from their defeated past and sometimes tragic present to overcome every obstacle that stood in their way.

Each of you, in your own specific way, is already a champion. I love each of you, and I know that you already know this, but your coaches believe in you, in your goodness, strength, perseverance and talent. All that is left is the doing, the final proof, the champion's word, the champion's goal, the champion's victory.

God Bless,
Coach a.

A Letter Regarding the Palace of Lost Fish

Sometimes, you know, the snow never falls forever
—James Welch

i want to find the purest fish
where fish began and bears
learned the rivers by name
because it was their giving that gave
the river it's name

the boy carried his fish
upon a silver stringer

a guitar at dusk
mosquitoes conduct the air
horses breathe along watery ditches
guitar and water
this is my memory   like a will i leave it

there are blue hearts on a cliff white
crosses on another   none are ancient
yet each timeless as ghosts of
guitar pressing against night in the east
a moon   gold as sheep eyes

the boy carried his fish
upon a silver stringer

the river does not forget nor do i
once   i was a boy and
my friend played guitar
echoing like gunshot against the
tiered dusk of summer days

something echoed from
an ancient part of him that was
palace to lost fish and
other dreams that escape the
hooks we substitute for love

the boy carried his fish
upon a silver stringer

and now almost all the poets i love
are dead and the one
i read tonight cannot
leave winter alone always
snow   the world bright as blindness

gunshot echoes white against
cliffs where once in an ancient
time   before people kept time
fish as pure as sound once swam

the boy carried his fish
upon a silver stringer

the river loves us   i love the river
once there was a boy and upon
a silver stringer were the fish of his dreams
the dreams of boys and loss
nothing melts when memory is involved

the river does not rise in
may as it should   june finds
water low and helicopters
come in the night to save
lives already lost

the boy carried his fish
upon a silver stringer

when fate was written
the rivers had yet
to carve canyons and perhaps
boys of an age like ours
boys that know the chords

of ditch water and river song at
the confluence of blood cliff   guitar
with raw instruments of bright day
might play for you and me too
a song only God and boys are capable of

the boy carried his fish
upon a silver stringer

this town is versed in the
art of things born dying
ancient fish that fed in the womb
their migration north to deep water
where once another boy drowned and

grown men with broken hearts
found him   eyes turned
toward the white sun of
lost words the priest wishes
he would have said to save you

the boy carried his fish
upon a silver stringer

on the streets we live for evidence
of our sanity   we stay vigilant as ravens
for drug deals and other fish that
flee to find a place where
fish are pure and memory

is not a haunting thing but
more like the wishes of bears   or is it men
for fish running so thick
men   or is it bears   can cross rivers
on the blue black wet flesh of fish

the boy carried his fish
upon a silver stringer

here is a prayer that bears can sleep for
two winters at a time   what haunts
the poet i read tonight is a
winter of loss   yet watery things
echo as if only the river lives